Three Essays in Law and Economics

Jeanne Mouton

Foreword by Frédéric Marty

Concurrences

2026

Paris – New York – London

106 West 32nd Street, Suite 144 New York, NY, 10001, USA
www.concurrences.com
book@concurrences.com

First Printing, June 2026
978-1-954750-93-7 (Paperback)
Library of Congress Control Number: 2026937246

Cover Design : Yves Buliard, www.yvesbuliard.fr
Book Design and Layout implementation: Nord Compo

Concurrences Books

Tributes

Huang Yong – Leading and Riding the Tide of China's Competition Law, *2025*

James F. Rill – A Life in Antitrust, *2024*

Eleanor M. Fox – Antitrust Ambassador to the World, *2021*

Herbert Hovenkamp – The Dean of American Antitrust Law, *2021*

Frédéric Jenny – Standing Up for Convergence and Relevance in Antitrust, (Vol. I & II), *2019 & 2021*

Albert Foer – A Consumer Voice in the Antitrust Arena, *2020*

Richard Whish – Taking Competition Law Outside the Box, *2020*

Douglas H. Ginsburg – An Antitrust Professor on the Bench (Vol. I & II), *2018 & 2020*

Wang Xiaoye – The Pioneer of Competition Law in China, *A. Emch, W. Ng (eds.), 2019*

Ian S. Forrester – A Scot without Borders (Vol. I & II), *A. Komninos (eds.), 2015*

William E. Kovacic – An Antitrust Tribute (Vol. I & II), *2013 & 2014*

Practical Books

Guide du droit polynésien de la concurrence, *W. Chaiehloudj, Y. Lecornu, J. Peyre, V. Terrien, (eds.), 2026*

Competition Law and the Challenges of Insular Economies – A Focus on French Polynesia and the Pacific Region, *J. Peyre, E. Silvestro, V. Terrien, T. Emen, Y. Lecornu (eds.), 2025*

Competition Inspections under EU Law, 2nd Edition, *N. Jalabert-Doury, 2025*

Navigating the DMA: Application Across National Jurisdictions, *G. Muscolo & A. Massolo (eds.), 2025*

Artificial Intelligence and Competition Policy, *A. Abbott, T. Schrepel (eds.), 2024*

State Aid & National Enforcement, *J. Derenne, D. Jouve, C. Lemaire, F. Martucci (eds.), 2024*

The 2023 U.S. Merger Guidelines: *A Review, Sean Sullivan (ed.), 2024*

Competition Inspections in 25 Jurisdictions 2nd Edition – A Practitioner's Guide, *N. Jalabert-Doury (ed.), 2024*

EU Antitrust Enforcement – Law, Economics, History, *Policy & Practice, Wouter P. J. Wils, 2024*

The EU Foreign Subsidies Regulation, *Andreas Reindl, Isabelle Van Damme, 2024*

Compendium of Antitrust Damages Actions – ICC – 2nd edition, *J.W.H. Denton AO, F. Brunet, S. Williams, C. Inthavisay (eds.), 2023*

Pharmaceutical Antitrust: An Analysis of US and EU Law, *M. Thill-Tayara, G. Gordon (eds.), 2023*

Innovation Paradox in Merger Control, *G. Gurkaynak, 2023*

Antitrust and the Digital Economy, *Y. Katsoulacos (ed.), 2023 (in collaboration with CRESSE)*

Judicial Review of Competition Cases, *D. Ginsburg, T. Eicke (eds.), 2023*

Competition Law Treatment of Joint Ventures, *B. Bleicher, N. Campbell, A. Hamilton, N. Hukkinen, A. Khan, A. Mordaunt (eds.), 2022 (in collaboration with the IBA)*

Information Exchange & Related Risks, *Z. Marosi, M. Soares (eds.), 2022 (in collaboration with the IBA)*

Rulemaking Authority of the US Federal Trade Commission, *D. Crane (ed.), 2022*

The International Competition Network at Twenty, *D. Anderson & P. Lugard (eds.), 2022*

Competition Case Law Digest – 5th Edition, *F. Jenny, N. Charbit (eds.), 2022*

Competition Inspections in 21 Jurisdictions – A Practitioner's Guide, *N. Jalabert-Doury (ed.), 2022*

Perspectives on Antitrust Compliance, *A. Riley, A. Stephan, A. Tubbs (eds.), 2022 (in collaboration with the ICC)*

Turkish Competition Law, *G. Gürkaynak, 2021*

Competition Law – Climate Change & Environmental Sustainability, *S. Holmes, D. Middelschulte, M. Snoep (eds.), 2021*

Merger Control in Latin America – A Jurisdictional Guide, *P. Burnier da Silveira, P. Sittenfeld (eds.), 2020*

Competition Inspections under EU Law – A Practitioner's Guide, *N. Jalabert-Doury, 2020*

Gun Jumping in Merger Control – A Jurisdictional Guide, *C. Hatton, Y. Comtois, A. Hamilton (eds.), 2019 (in collaboration with the IBA)*

Choice – A New Standard for Competition Analysis? *P. Nihoul (ed.), 2016*

PhD Theses

FRAND Licensing: a comparative study of the interactions between competition law and the law of obligations, *H. Cowderoy (2026)*

Intent in Competition Law, *M.S. Garnier, 2025*

Three Essays in Law and Economics: Digital Markets and Abuse of Dominance, *J. Mouton, 2025*

The Economics of Digital Markets – Essays in Theoretical and Empirical Industrial Organization, *E. Arnaud-Joufray, 2024*

Abuse of Platform Power, *F. Bostoen, 2023*

Reform of Chinese State-Owned Enterprises, *X. Bai, 2023*

Competition & Regulation in Network Industries – Essays in Industrial Organization, *J-M. Zogheib, 2021*

The Role of Media Pluralism in the Enforcement of EU Competition Law, *K. Bania, 2019*

Buyer Power, *I. Herrera Anchustegui, 2017*

TABLE OF CONTENTS

FOREWORD

The present work constitutes a revised and expanded version of Jeanne Mouton's doctoral dissertation. This book lies at the intersection of two fields: the economics of competition law and industrial organization applied to digital markets. It addresses the sanctioning of unilateral conduct by dominant firms and examines the effectiveness of the various instruments available to competition authorities.

Jeanne Mouton's piece achieves a remarkable synthesis by combining multiple economic methods (econometrics, game theory, and data science) to tackle two fundamental questions in competition law: how to deter, prevent, and remedy the effects of anticompetitive practices, and, in the latter case, how to ensure the effectiveness of remedies. The three chapters that compose her book successively illuminate these dimensions.

The first chapter sits at the crossroads of remediation and deterrence. Drawing on an original dataset compiling decisions from several European Union Member States, it identifies the determinants of successful damages actions in cases involving unilateral conduct. The issue of private enforcement is crucial, both as a complement to public enforcement where the latter may be lacking, and as a means of strengthening the deterrent effect of competition law sanctions.

The second chapter contributes to a broader diversification of competition policy tools aimed at preventing harm arising from the concentration of economic power. The focus shifts here from the sufficiency of ex post sanctions to the prevention of anticompetitive conduct. The analysis centers on anti-steering provisions under the European Digital Markets Act. Departing from an econometric approach, the chapter relies on formal modelling to demonstrate how ex ante rules introduced by the DMA may alter the incentives of market participants.

The third chapter explores a further avenue for enhancing the effectiveness of competition rules through negotiated procedures. It draws on the European Commission's December 2022 decision concerning Amazon to assess the impact of the remedies proposed in response to concerns over self-preferencing practices affecting algorithmic ranking.

The dissertation, of which this book is the product, addresses a crucial question faced by public enforcers before engaging in competition litigation: if a practice is found to be anticompetitive, will the resulting decision be sufficiently deterrent and capable of restoring competitive conditions? In other words, absent the ability to design effective remedies, can antitrust enforcement be considered effective?

As this work demonstrates, this issue is particularly acute in digital markets. Sanctions may be under-deterrent and perceived as a mere cost of doing business; the net effects of the conduct are especially difficult to assess, given the complexity of balancing competing impacts; and the design and implementation of remedies capable of restoring competition pose significant challenges.

To address these difficulties, Jeanne Mouton's dissertation puts forward three complementary instruments: damages actions, which enhance deterrence while providing compensation to injured parties; commitment procedures, which enable the rapid cessation of potentially irreversible harm and the implementation of effective remedies; and ex ante regulation, aimed at preventing competitive harm that cannot be adequately corrected ex post.

One of the central strengths of this work lies in its systematic reflection on the conditions for effectiveness and on the impacts of these various tools, combining legal and economic analysis while mobilizing the full range of the economist's toolkit: econometrics, data science, and microeconomic modelling.

This achievement is the result of sustained effort and exceptional perseverance, as well as an original academic trajectory and remarkable personal and professional qualities. Jeanne Mouton's academic path is distinguished by a transition from law to economics (rather than the reverse), made possible by outstanding intellectual curiosity and a willingness to take significant risks during both her master's studies and doctoral research. Her ability to master both disciplines with equal rigor has also been fostered by professional experience pursued alongside her doctoral work, successively at *Concurrences*, the College of Europe, and currently at the European Commission.

The most striking manifestation of these qualities, and of her ability to work collaboratively, lies in the research partnerships developed during the preparation of the dissertation. A collaboration with Christian Rüsche on anti-steering provisions, mobilizing game-theoretic tools, resulted in a joint publication in the *European Journal of Law and Economics*, from which Chapter II of this book is derived. A second collaboration with Benoît Rottembourg (INRIA) on self-preferencing enabled the use of data science techniques to assess the impact of remedies resulting from negotiated procedures. The outcomes of this collaboration are compellingly set out in Chapter III. Finally, ongoing work with Ilona Dielen, also a recent PhD graduate from our research team, extends the analysis presented in Chapter I and will allow for an even more refined econometric assessment of follow-on damages actions under Article 102 TFEU.

These collaborations testify to Jeanne Mouton's ability to develop collective research projects and to share her intellectual enthusiasm and scientific curiosity. From the outset of her doctoral studies, she has been a key member of our research and teaching team (Competition, Public Policies, and Sector Specific Regulations (Ccorsé) within the Research Group on Law, Economics and Management (GREDEG, CNRS – Université Côte d'Azur)), despite geographical distance and demanding professional commitments. She has played a central role in fostering collective research initiatives among members of the Sophia-Antipolis-based community of industrial organization and competition economics, while also building strong connections with legal scholars in economic law, both in competition and digital regulation, as well as with colleagues at INRIA.

Supervising this dissertation has therefore been an ideal experience for a doctoral advisor, and it is a privilege to write the preface to such comprehensive and rigorous work. I can only express my gratitude to Jeanne for her contribution to the collective dynamics of our research team and my firm conviction that her trajectory within the antitrust community, still at a (brilliant) early stage, holds the promise of an outstanding career.

Toulouse, 18 march 2026

Frédéric MARTY
CNRS Research Director
UMR 7321 GREDEG – CNRS / Côte d'Azur University

À mon père,

INTRODUCTION

1. This dissertation consists of three essays that fall under the broad banner of competition law and economics. Each essay corresponds to one chapter and answers a research question under different angles of economics of litigation studying unilateral conducts from a dominant player causing competitive damage.[1] This dissertation deals with the compensation, prevention, and remediation of that damage, with different perspectives and tools, combining methods from data analysis, econometrics, and game theory. The first essay relates to the private enforcement of litigation, with the aim to compensate for damage. The second essay relates to the regulatory approach, whether damage on the market can be prevented with *ex-ante* rules and obligations. The third essay relates to antitrust commitment decisions and the auditability of those remedies when it comes to opaque ranking algorithms.

2. The general aim of the dissertation is to compare the benefits and hurdles of complementary tools to traditional public enforcement of competition law in digital markets. First, private enforcement or damages actions are intended to complement public enforcement of competition law but were originally conceived in the context of cartels. However, infringements on digital markets are mainly infringements of Article 102 TFEU. Second, the Digital Markets Act is a regulation specific to the digital sector, which imposes *ex-ante* rules on gatekeepers and clearly aims to increase the effectiveness of enforcement compared to competition law enforcement. Finally, commitment decisions are one of the tools of competition law public enforcement wherein the undertaking offers the commitments; the whole procedure is quicker than an infringement procedure and does not establish the company's liability. It is questioned whether commitment decisions are an effective tool in digital markets and whether the implementation of agreed commitments can be effectively audited. Consequently, the economic analysis of alternatives to traditional public enforcement of competition law in digital markets will allow us to reflect on policy recommendations in the context of a global enforcement system strategy in digital markets.

3. The first essay studies the determinants of a successful private enforcement action following an abuse of dominant position. The literature on private enforcement is mainly focused on damages actions following cartel infringements, which is aligned with the broader picture that in EU competition law there are more private enforcement cases following infringements of Article 101 TFEU, than for infringements of Article 102

1 Each essay is accompanied by a dedicated bibliography to facilitate the reading considering that each essay can be read independently.

TFEU. Therefore, this essay aims to fill the gap in the empirical literature on damages actions for abuse of dominance position with the policy perspective of the upcoming damages actions in digital markets. To do so, this essay relies on an original database of 194 cases from France, the United Kingdom, and Italy, and empirically analyses the determinants of successful private enforcement actions following an abuse of dominance. The discussion section closes on the specific hurdles of private enforcement in digital markets, considering the complexity of these infringements, with an analysis of the damages claims in the database following the Google Shopping case.

4. The second essay studies anti-steering clauses in digital markets under the framework of a digital sector specific regulation. The Digital Markets Act (DMA), a digital sector specific regulation, aims to complement the enforcement of competition law on dominant players in the digital market with *ex-ante* rules on designated gatekeepers. Considering how recent the regulation is, with the first gatekeepers being designated in September 2023, there is not much economics literature analysing the potential effects of the rules in the Regulation. This essay focuses on Article 5(4) of the DMA, which prohibits anti-steering clauses, and relies on game theory to explore the potential changes of incentives for different business models after the introduction of the obligation.

5. The third essay starts with a commitment decision from the EU Commission, the Amazon Buy Box case, imposing remedies on an e-commerce platform to study the effectiveness and auditability of remedies imposed on a ranking algorithm. This essay fits into the literature of choice ranking, product prominence and the nascent specific literature on Amazon's Buy Box and adds to the literature in terms of context and in terms of method. This essay does not only study the determinants of the winner of Amazon's Buy Box, but rather, whether the remedies imposed on the Buy Box had the effect expected. In terms of method, this essay relies on several methods, from a logistical regression to "less explainable" models (ensemble methods like random forest and gradient boosting), to demonstrate the added value of using more sophisticated technologies.

6. The concept of abuse of dominance in the European Union (EU), as well as the main characteristics of digital markets, are the pillars on which each essay of this dissertation builds upon.

7. Abuse of dominance is sanctioned by Article 102 on the Treaty of the Functioning of the European Union (TFEU). Dominance in itself is not sanctioned. Dominant firms can compete on the merits. However dominant firms have a special responsibility not to abuse their dominant position. Article 102 TFEU provides a non-exhaustive list of elements that may constitute an abuse of dominance. In 2008 the EU Commission

published a communication Guidance on the Commission's enforcement priorities in applying Article 82 of the EC Treaty to abusive exclusionary conduct by dominant undertakings. While an abuse of dominance can either take the form of exclusionary or exploitative conduct, the communication from 2008 expressly took the position of prioritising the sanction of exclusionary behaviours. Commenting on this communication, Akman (2009) argues that Article 82 EC has been wrongly narrowed down and should recognise exploitative abuse, especially excessive pricing, as a central and legitimate form of abuse of dominance.

8. In March 2023, the EU Commission announced new guidelines on exclusionary abuses and published a communication amending its 2008 guidance enforcement priorities for exclusionary conducts. The aim of the Communication was to reflect on the evolution of the Commission's enforcement priorities over time, on the effects-based approach to Article 102 as confirmed by the Union Courts, and on the clarification of the meaning and scope of the concepts set out in the Guidance on enforcement priorities.[2] The Policy Brief accompanying the new guidelines[3] puts the emphasis on embracing the dynamic nature of competition and providing a "workable basis for vigorous enforcement" of Article 102.

9. The number of investigations for abuse of dominance is "far more modest" in comparison to merger transactions (OECD, 2022).[4] This can be explained not only by the complexity of detecting an abuse of dominance but also by the difficulty to fit a sanction. An abuse of dominance can either be sanctioned through the lens of public enforcement or private enforcement. Where public enforcement proceedings may result in administrative sanctions or the imposition of binding remedies (with or without a finding of infringement), private enforcement proceedings may result in the award of compensatory damages.

10. One of the six priorities of the EU Commission for 2019/2024 is a Europe fit for the digital age, focusing on three key objectives in digital markets: technology that works for people, a fair and competitive economy, and an open, democratic, and sustainable society. The Commissioner for Competition, Vestager, is setting the strategic direction and chairing the Commissioner's Group on a Europe fit for the digital age. Member States' competition authorities have also made the enforcement of competition in digital markets a priority. Therefore, at the EU level, there is a coordinated

---

2 EU Commission, Press release, "Antitrust: Commission announces new guidelines on exclusionary abuses and amends guidance on enforcement priorities", 27 March 2023, available at: https://ec.europa.eu/commission/presscorner/detail/en/IP_23_1911.

3 EU Commission, Competition Policy Brief, "A dynamic and workable effects-based approach to abuse of dominance", Issue 1, March 2023, ISBN 978-92-68-01420-2, ISSN: 2315-3113.

4 The OECD launched in 2018 the CompStats OECD database, providing general statistics relating to competition agencies, including data on enforcement. The OECD Competition trends report from 2023 provides, among other metrics, the average number of cartel decisions and the average number of abuse of dominance decisions per region.

public enforcement effort to monitor dominant players in digital markets, in case they abuse their dominant position.

11. In October 2022, the Digital Markets Act was published in the Office Journal of the EU. The DMA is a sector-specific regulation, setting out clear obligations and prohibitions, which are enforced for designated gatekeepers. Some of the obligations and prohibitions have been "inspired" by past abuse of dominance cases. The enforcement of its *ex-ante* rules aims to complement the enforcement of competition law on dominant players in digital markets.

12. Departing from the classic approach of competition in the market, the specific characteristics of the digital sector led to "competition for the market" dynamic. The two concepts were already distinguished in the frame of the Microsoft case.[5] Geroski (2003), studying the Microsoft case, distinguishes competition in the market as competition between firms operating the same standard, and competition for the market, as competition between standards.

13. The Crémer report (2020) was commissioned by Commissioner Vestager with the goal "to explore how competition policy should evolve to continue to promote pro-consumer innovation in the digital age". The report identifies some specific competitive risks for digital markets, for example the risk of "cannibalisation effect" in tech acquisitions. Crémer et al. (2020), highlighted the main characteristics of digital markets and their challenges for competition policy. The authors focused on three key characteristics of the digital economy: extreme returns to scale, network externalities, and the role of data. The three key characteristics combined lead to concentrated markets with a few players.

14. The business models and economics of platforms have been studied by Rochet and Tirole (2003, 2004, 2006) and Jullien and Sand-Zantman (2021). Rochet and Tirole (2006) define a two-sided market "if the platform can affect the volume of transactions by charging more to one side of the market and reducing the price paid by the other side by an equal amount; in other words, the price structure matters, and platforms must design it so as to bring both sides on board". Jullien and Sand-Zantman (2021) discuss the specific new issues raised by platforms for competition policy in comparison to "traditional markets".

15. Belleflamme and Peitz (2021) discuss in depth the interaction between the platform and their users when there is an attraction spiral: a higher level of interaction in one group makes it more attractive for the other group. The authors distinguish between within-group and cross-group network effects. Regarding the impact of data in digital markets, Pino (2022) offers an exhaustive literature review structured around three classes of

5 T-201/04 – Microsoft v Commission.

models, depending on the business model's approach to data collection: data acquisition with no strategic interaction, data collected from consumers, and data collected from intermediaries.

16. The specific risks that digital markets present for competition policy raised the question of whether classic competition law provisions can meet these challenges. Caffarra (2019) takes the stance of relying on already existing theories of harm to sanction infringements in digital markets. Caffara emphasizes the need "to follow the money", meaning, to better understand the business models, differentiating between aggregators and platforms, as a solid prerequisite to enforcing competition law in digital markets. The OECD, in a 2020 report, also relates a list of potential observed conducts and market outcomes to existing theories of harm regarding the abuse of dominance.

17. Theoretically, classic competition law rules seemed to be "enough" to tackle abuse of dominance in digital markets. However, the recent public enforcement in digital markets has shown weaknesses, with lengthy and resource-intensive abuse of dominance cases.

18. Private parties are unlikely to have access to the same resources as competition authorities when bringing a claim for damages. This raises the questions of what determines the success of a private enforcement action and what lessons can be drawn for future claims in digital markets. (Essay 1)

19. Acknowledging that lengthy competition public enforcement is damaging both for business users and end users, the *ex-ante* rules designed by the Digital Markets Act are promising. Taking the specific example of anti-steering clauses, what could be the effects of the prohibition of these clauses by the DMA on the incentives for platform and business users? (Essay 2)

20. Faster public enforcement of competition law can be achieved through commitments and decisions, hence without sanctioning the undertaking. Following Amazon's Buy Box antitrust commitment decision, is it possible to effectively audit remedies facing opaque ranking algorithms? (Essay 3)

21. Having outlined the scope of the dissertation – which examines the benefits and challenges of private enforcement, the Digital Markets Act, and commitment decisions as complements to traditional public enforcement of unilateral conduct – and established their complementarity within a global enforcement model in digital markets, I now turn to each essay. For each, I present the specific research question addressed, its relevance, the gap in the literature it aims to fill, and the legal and economic tools selected to achieve the expected results.

22. The first essay aims to measure the determinants of successful EU competition damages actions following abuse of dominance infringements with the perspective of the upcoming damages claims in digital markets.

23. In EU competition law, public and private actions do not serve the same purpose. On the one hand, public action sanctions damage to the economy, while on the other, private action compensates for individual loss. Public action makes an overall assessment of the potential effects of the damage, which corresponds to the loss of surplus suffered by all market operators, competing undertakings, suppliers or applicants. Private parties pursue an objective of compensation when bringing a damages action; this does not imply that such actions lack a dissuasive effect, but rather that the dissuasive effect is not a motivating factor in the decision to initiate a claim.

24. Competition law damages actions in EU law were first formally established in case law, before being reformed with Directive 2014/104/EU, known as the Damages Directive. The BRT and Sabam judgments[6] established the direct effect of the articles finding breaches of competition law in the TFEU. The Courage and Crehan[7], and Manfredi[8] judgments clarified the scope of this direct effect.[9]

25. In June 2013, the EU Commission paired its proposal for a Damages Directive with a study on the impact of damages actions in competition law, including an assessment of the costs of the situation in 2013. The study estimated the cost of the ineffectiveness of private actions at €23 billion in terms of compensation foregone by victims each year in the European Union. The European Parliament approved the proposal on 17 April 2014. The Directive was then adopted by the Council on 10 November 2014 and published in the Official Journal on 5 December 2014, establishing 27 December 2016 as the deadline for Member States to transpose the legal instrument.

26. Based on the finding of an inequitable situation on the market regarding actions for damages, and to foster undistorted competition in the internal market, Directive 2014/104/EU states in Article 1 that its purpose is "to ensure that anyone who has suffered harm caused by an infringement of competition law by an undertaking or by an association of undertakings can effectively exercise the right to claim full compensation for that harm from that undertaking or association". The aim of the Damages Directive is to ensure a fine-tuned interaction between public and private action. In doing so, it needed to strike a balance between maintaining incentives for leniency programmes and settlement procedures and ensuring the right

---

6 BRT and SABAM, C-127/73.

7 Courage and Crehan, C-453/99.

8 Manfredi et autres, C-295/04.

9 Other rulings by the Court of Justice of the European Union have subsequently clarified private competitive action, including the Pfleiderer (C-360/09), Otis (C-199/01) and EnBW Energie (C-365/12P) rulings. During the transition period from these rulings to the Damages Directive, the European Commission also produced soft law instruments. In particular, the Green Paper on damages actions for breach of EU law, which identified the main obstacles to effective compensation, the White Paper on damages actions for breach of EU competition law, which put forward a number of suggestions to overcome the obstacles identified, and finally, a guide of non-binding guidelines for the Courts on the quantification of competitive damages.

to full compensation, all within the broader objective of deterring competition law infringements.

27. The purpose of this essay is to investigate the determinants of a successful action for damages following an abuse of dominance. Damages actions for breaches of Article 102 TFEU have been less studied in the literature and are the subject of limited case law. Intuitively, it seems that abuse of dominance infringements are more difficult for private claimants to characterise and quantify.

28. The research question is the following: what are the determinants of a successful damages action following an abuse of dominance?

29. The interest of this research question is twofold.

30. First, the limited empirical literature covering private enforcement of competition law in the EU is limited, and even more so when it comes to private enforcement following an abuse of dominance. In comparison with the EU competition law damages actions, the US antitrust private enforcement is directly designed to deter anticompetitive behaviour. Therefore, given its richer history of litigation, there is a richer literature on the US antitrust private enforcement. For example, Lande and Davis (2008, 2013) studied a selection of the most recent and largest US private enforcement cases. The authors compared the deterrence effect between private enforcement and federal criminal enforcement of antitrust laws. To do so, they compared, for the same cases, the amount paid in private litigation to the amount paid in criminal fines.

31. From the EU perspective, the empirical study of private enforcement are papers mapping damages actions with descriptive statistics, country wide or limited to a type of infringement. Rodger (2009, 2015), in a context of efforts to develop private enforcement, provides a comprehensive analysis of all competition law litigation in United Kingdom (UK) Courts, involving both breaches of EU and UK competition law. The author highlights descriptive statistics on the frequency of competition litigation, success rate, frequency of litigation before different Courts, and frequency of competition follow-on action. Ultimately, Rodger observes an increase in the success rate of private enforcement. The same way Rodger studied private enforcement from a country wide perspective, in the UK; Peyer (2012) empirically studied private enforcement in Germany and Sousa Ferro (2016) built a comprehensive overview of competition law damages case-law in Portugal. To this day, there is only one EU wide study of private enforcement, restricted to infringements of Article 101 of the TFEU. Laborde (2021)[10] built a comprehensive review of judgements, by national courts, on cartel damages claims at the EU level, covering 299 cases in the 2021 edition. The author measures the damages awards, with range

10 The first study dates back from 2016.

of overcharges, and the methods of quantification were relied upon in the cases. The studies from Laborde focus on cartel damages claims.

32. At the time of the inception of the Directive 2014/104/EU private enforcement of cartel infringements was a priority, deemed as the most harmful practice[11]. However, the recent fines in administrative sanctions in digital markets[12] require the attention of the policymaker. Infringements to competition law in digital markets can result in widespread harmful practices for the small and medium business partners of the eco-system and for consumers. On the one hand, small and medium enterprises may fear exclusion from the platform and therefore have low incentives to introduce a damages action. On the other hand, consumers may face difficulties in the identification of harmful practices, in the quantification of harm, and therefore in recovering damages.

33. Leading to the second interest in our research question, the first essay aims to fill in the literature gap on damages actions for abuse of dominance position with the policy perspective of the upcoming damages actions in digital markets.

34. Digital markets have given rise to complex infringements, prompting discussions on the potential need to reform competition law provisions and exacerbating the asymmetry of information between dominant eco-systems and their business users and end consumers. Therefore, one could expect private parties to lose their information advantage when introducing damages claim following an infringement on digital markets.[13] This would not be the only hurdle they would face, as Newman (2016) outlined the challenges for private enforcement in zero-priced markets, from a US antitrust perspective. Among these challenges, the author stresses the increasing complexity of proofs needed by customers seeking damages for 'attentional' or 'informational' overcharges.

35. In terms of method, not only has this research question not yet been covered by literature, but most economic studies of private enforcement are papers mapping damages actions with descriptive statistics, country wide or limited to a type of infringement. Thus, the originality of this essay lies both in its original database covering three countries and, in its

---

11 Connor and Lande (2008) issued a quantification study for Oxera providing a database on cartel overcharges. The authors found overcharges in 93% of the cases in their samples, with an overcharge between 20 and 23%. This estimation was then corrected for biases and potential errors by Boyer and Kotchoni (2011) finding a mean overcharge of all cartel cases of 17,5% with a median of 14%. The EU Commission staff working document impact assessment report on damages actions for breach of the EU antitrust rules (2013) rely on these studies to consider as an option a rebuttable presumption of harm for cartel infringements.

12 Taking the sole example of Google, the EU General Court confirming the fine imposed by the EU Commission against the firm for € 2.42 billion in the Google Shopping case; the General Court slightly decrease the first instance fine and imposed a € 4.125 billion fine in the Google Android case; and Google appealed the € 1.49 billion fine imposed by the EU Commission in the Google AdSense case.

13 Following the reasoning from Segal and Whinston (2006) if the infringement is complex and requires knowledge of economics and market conditions, private parties lose their informational advantage in favour of public authorities and their experts.

methodology, which is similar to two empirical studies on public application of competition law. The first paper, Lauke (2003), studies whether antitrust decisions can be explained by knowledge of the allegations and some observable market structure characteristics, relying on a dataset of decisions from the German Federal Cartel Office. The second paper, from Janin and Menoni (2007), is an empirical analysis of the opinions in merger cases from the Conseil de la Concurrence, studying the factors explaining the rulings. Both papers analyse a binary outcome, with either a logit or a probit model, on a limited number of (decisions) observations.

36. The original dataset covers 194 cases, from France, Italy, and the United Kingdom, from 1988 to 2022. This essay analyses the determinants of a successful damages action using a logit model. The outcome is coded as positive if the private parties receive compensation for their harm, if their request for an injunction is granted, if the case is closed with a settlement agreement, or if liability is established. Several hypotheses are tested: whether a follow-on case has a greater chance of success than a stand-alone case; whether claimants seeking injunctions, as opposed to monetary damages, are more likely to obtain a successful outcome; whether the introduction of the Damages Directive positively affects case success; whether success rates vary depending on the sector in which the abuse of dominance occurred; and whether damages claims have a lower probability of success in the digital sector.

37. The results show indications that follow-on actions are less likely to be successful than stand-alone cases, which is surprising and indicates a difference in litigation of damages actions between infringements to Article 101 and 102 TFEU. Second, cases in which injunctions were sought do not have more chances of success compared to cases in which monetary damages were sought (noting that these are not exclusive strategies). Third, the chances of success for damages claims have increased since the entry and end date of implementation of the Damages Directive. Fourth, while measuring the effects of economic sectors, only the sectors of information and communication and transportation are statistically significant with a negative sign. Finally, introducing a claim for damages in digital markets decreases the chances of success and this effect is amplified if the claim was introduced in France.

38. The discussion section closes on the specific hurdles of private enforcement in digital markets, considering the complexity of these infringements, with an analysis of the damages claims in the dataset, in the UK, France, and Italy, following the Google Shopping case.

39. The Google Shopping case[14] is a case study of a complicated and lengthy public enforcement of competition law, which is raising difficulties for follow-on private enforcement. Interestingly, the Google Shopping case can also relate to the second essay of the thesis. Indeed, some of

14 AT.39740.

the Digital Markets Act's obligations are closely related to major past and on-going infringement cases of competition law in digital markets (Petit, 2021), including the Google Shopping case with the prohibition of self-preferencing. It is without surprise, that there is a strong interplay between the DMA and the enforcement of competition law, as formalised in recital 10 of the DMA, which states that "this Regulation aims to complement the enforcement of competition law". Additionally, Recital 11 highlights the difference and complementarity of goals between competition law enforcement and the application of the DMA:

"Articles 101 and 102 TFEU and the corresponding national competition rules concerning anticompetitive multilateral and unilateral conduct as well as merger control have as their objective the protection of undistorted competition on the market. This Regulation pursues an objective that is complementary to, but different from that of protecting undistorted competition on any given market, as defined in competition-law terms, which is to ensure that markets where gatekeepers are present are and remain contestable and fair, independently from the actual, potential or presumed effects of the conduct of a given gatekeeper covered by this Regulation on competition on a given market. This Regulation therefore aims to protect a different legal interest from that protected by those rules and it should apply without prejudice to their application."

40. The second essay, co-authored with Dr. Christian Rusche,[15] aims to provide a legal and economic assessment of a specific provision of the DMA.[16] The DMA is a sector-specific regulation, published in the Official Journal of the European Union on 12 October 2022, introducing rules for platforms designated as "gatekeepers" in the digital sector. The DMA is part of the Digital Services Act package, together with the Digital Services Act (DSA), with two main goals: creating a safer digital space where fundamental rights of digital users are protected (DSA) and establishing a level playing field fostering innovation, growth, and competitiveness in the European Single Market (DMA).

41. The DMA arose out of concerns that a "small number of large undertakings providing core platform services have emerged with considerable economic power that could qualify them to be designated as gatekeepers pursuant to this Regulation" (Recital 2). The Regulation set rules with the goals "to ensure contestability and fairness for the markets in the digital sector" (Recital 7) in the EU, for both the "benefits of the business users and end users" (Art 1). The Regulation targets "gatekeepers," designated in accordance with the quantitative and qualitative criteria set out in Article 3.The designation refers to the provider's core platform services. The services that are core platform

15 Economist, Institut der Deutschen Wirtschaft (IW).

16 This essay was published in the European Journal of Law & Economics on the 26th of October 2023.

services are listed in Article 2(2) of the DMA. When designated, a gatekeeper should comply with all obligations contained in Art 5, 6 and 7 with respect to its core platform services listed in the designation decision. The obligations contained in Art 5 are directly applicable to the gatekeeper, while the obligations contained in Art 6 and 7 can be subject to further specification.

42. This essay focused on one specific provision in the DMA: the prohibition for gatekeepers to impose anti-steering clauses. The DMA impact assessment defines an anti-steering clause as one that prevents business users of the gatekeeper from "directing acquired consumers to offers other than those provided on the platform, even though such alternative offers may be cheaper or otherwise potentially more attractive."

43. The anti-steering clauses were observed in vertically integrated platforms, for example, in Apple's App Store or Google's Play Store. We chose to focus on the anti-steering provision of the DMA for two reasons. First, because it relates to several on-going competition cases, and second, because anti-steering clauses are often linked with a proportional fee imposed by the platforms on their business users. Additionally, compared to the on-going App Store case, the core platform services, as defined by the DMA, are wider than the market definition set by the EU Commission case law (market for the distribution of music streaming apps through its App Store). Hence, the impact of the implementation of the obligation should have a larger effect than a case-by-case competition law enforcement.

44. The research question is the following: Does Art 5(4) of the DMA incentivise gatekeepers to adapt their business model and do business users benefit and/or also modify their own business model?

45. The EU Commission sent a statement of objection to Apple, in April 2021[17] and in February 2023.[18] In its 2021 Statement of Objection, the EU Commission addressed two specific rules: the mandatory use of Apple's In-App Purchase (IAP), enabling Apple to charge a 30% commission on all subscriptions acquired via the IAP, and the anti-steering provisions, which limit app developers' capacity to inform users of alternative purchasing options. The preliminary view of the EU Commission was that these rules imposed by Apple could distort the competition in the market for music streaming services by raising the costs of competing music streaming app developers, having the effect of leading to higher prices for consumers since the investigation showed that most streaming providers passed this fee on to end users. In the 2023 statement of objection, the Commission "does no longer take a position as to the legality of the IAP obligation for the purposes of this antitrust investigation but rather focuses on the contractual restrictions that Apple imposed on app developers which prevent them from informing

17 Press release: https://ec.europa.eu/commission/presscorner/detail/en/ip_21_2061.

18 Press release: https://ec.europa.eu/commission/presscorner/detail/en/ip_23_1217.

iPhone and iPad users of alternative music subscription options at lower prices outside of the app and to effectively choose those." The EU Commission re-prioritised its investigation to solely focus on the anti-steering clause.

46. As illustrated by the App Store case, anti-steering clauses have been observed in vertically integrated platforms, where the platform imposes a proportional fee on app developers. Muthers and Wismer (2012) develop a model to compare the preferences of the dominant intermediary and sellers, as well as the resulting market outcomes for membership fees, per-transaction fees, and proportional fees. The authors find that the intermediary's opportunity to compete with sellers and the magnitude of its production costs influence the trade-off between different types of fees charged to sellers. Proportional fees mitigate the threat of entry from the intermediary, while preserving sellers' investment incentives.

47. There is not an explicit provision regulating fees imposed by gatekeepers under the DMA, therefore, the anti-steering clauses, tied with proportional fees imposed on sellers, is an example of the need for a parallel enforcement of the DMA and competition law.

48. While the DMA only started applying as of the beginning of May 2023, there is already some literature critically assessing the framework of the regulation (Petit, 2021; Petit and Moreno, 2023; Colangelo, 2023) as well as its interplay with competition law (Komninos, 2022; Andriychuk, 2023). Among all the obligations of the DMA, it seems that the self-preferencing practice has captured a wide share of the attention in the literature (Bougette et al., 2022; Bougette et al., 2022; Peitz, 2023; and Kittaka et al. 2023 for a literature review on self-preferencing by platforms). The role of economics in the implementation of the DMA has also been discussed, since the DMA is a regulation with *ex-ante* obligations applied to gatekeepers with no by-effect assessment or discussion on the potential efficiencies[19]. Gallagher and Abecasis (2022) discuss the consequences of removing economic considerations from the DMA implementation, with a risk of under- and over-enforcement and restricted ability to be future proof. Nonetheless, the authors expect economic analysis to be required to ensure the objective of "contestability", which refers to an economic concept. Additionally, economic analysis should be important as regards to obligations where gatekeepers receive compensation for the services or data they must provide. Fletcher et al. (2023) identifies six contexts in which economics can play a role in the implementation of the DMA.

49. In this essay, we study a specific prohibition in the DMA, with parallel competition law enforcement. Decarolis and Li (2022) follow a similar approach in their study of the Google Android case. The authors identified

19 Recital 23 of the DMA: "Any justification on economic grounds seeking to enter into market definition or to demonstrate efficiencies deriving from a specific type of behaviour by the undertaking providing core platform services should be discarded, as it is not relevant to the designation as a gatekeeper."

three relevant dimensions of the DMA and rely on a model to demonstrate how the enforcement of these dimensions can result in a greater impact on online search engine markets, increasing the number of potential users of competing search engines.

50. Chapter Two examines the prohibition of anti-steering clauses under the DMA. Given the absence of a dedicated literature on anti-steering clauses, we treat them as a form of mixed bundling, thereby connecting the discussion to the existing literature on tying and bundling (Choi, 2010; Rochet and Tirole, 2008; Sun, 2018; Lin et al., 2020).

51. The EU Commission Joint Research Center report, from a panel of economic experts on the DMA, expressly touches upon the anti-steering clause prohibition in the DMA. According to economic experts, the possibility for service providers to route payments through their own websites may, for developers, create an incentive to reduce app download prices. However, app stores being deprived of aftermarket revenues may compensate by increasing market entry prices for app uploads and reviews (Cabral et al., 2021).

52. In our game theory model, the market can be described using the Hotelling (1929) model. Several authors have already relied on the Hotelling model to model firms' interactions in two-sided markets (Spulber, 1999; Alexandrov et al., 2011). We analyse the changes in incentives for platform and business users following the introduction of the obligation. Our model allows us to study the payoff and data of the platform and the reaction of business users to join the platform or not, following the introduction of the obligation. Regarding the decision of the platform to impose a fee, we differentiate between two cases: whether all business users were already on the platform and whether not all business users were using the platform before the introduction of the obligation.

53. Assuming that the total amount of consumers in e-commerce is constant, five potential effects can be drawn from the results of our model:

    (a) Using the platform becomes more attractive to business users.

    (b) The obligation is attractive as well and therefore, relied upon by business users. In order to do so, they might even open an independent web shop.

    (c) The platform has an incentive to become vertically integrated.

    (d) The amount of data available for business users and the platform is likely to increase.

    (e) Following the introduction of the obligation, fees are likely to increase if all business users were already using the platform before.

    (f) Otherwise, the effect of the obligation on the amount of the fee is indeterminate and depends on the specific manifestation of the variables.

54. Based on these results, we provide policy recommendations, including the recommendation not to reduce competition law enforcement efforts, as not all anticompetitive effects associated with anti-steering clauses are covered by the DMA.

55. The third essay is likewise situated in digital markets and focuses on a competition law case concerning a vertically integrated dominant undertaking. The second essay analyses how such a firm may abuse its dominant position by imposing anti-steering clauses and proportional fees on its business users, leading to higher costs for app developers and higher prices for end users.

56. The third essay studies how a vertically integrated platform can abuse its dominant position through product prominence and discriminatory practices. In the latter case study, the platform designs the rules of the winner of the Buy-Box algorithm to prominently display its own results, resulting in self-preferencing practices.

57. The third chapter is co-authored with Benoît Rottembourg[20] and contributes to the debate of auditing algorithms, in the framework of an antitrust commitment decision. This essay is a case study of the decision from the EU Commission in December 2022 to impose remedies on Amazon's Buy Box.

58. The Buy Box is the item displayed on the detailed page of a product for sale on the Amazon platform, located next to the "Add to basket" button. The Buy Box prominently displays the offer of one single seller. When a seller wins the Buy box, the seller appears as the default choice seller on the product page. While Amazon's website only mentions the increased chance of selling an item when it appears in the buy box, 80% of sales are said to go through the Buy Box, making it unavoidable. Although Amazon presented the criteria of selection of the winner as simple and transparent, the Buy Box has been the subject of numerous competitive disputes on both sides of the Atlantic.

59. The research question is the following: is it possible to audit the ranking strategy of the algorithm of an online platform, via data scraping on a price tracker and machine learning?

60. This essay studies the effectiveness of remedies imposed by a regulator, taking the specific example of algorithmic auditing. Our interest in this decision relates to the EU Commission decision to impose remedies on Amazon's Buy Box. The EU Commission opened a formal investigation in November 2020[21] under the concerns over a possible bias in granting sellers' access to its Buy Box, leading to a preferential treatment of

---

20 Institut National de Recherche en Sciences et Technologies du Numérique (INRIA), Head of the Pilot Project *Regalia*.

21 Press release: https://ec.europa.eu/commission/presscorner/detail/en/ip_20_2077.

Amazon's own retail business and sellers using Amazon's logistics and delivery services. On December 2022,[22] the EU Commission accepted commitments from Amazon to treat all sellers equally when ranking the offers for the purposes of the selection of the Buy Box winner.

61. Now that the commitments have been agreed, how can compliance be ensured?

62. Regulation 1/2003 introduced formal remedies proceedings in competition law, with the aim of ensuring easier litigation. There are two situations in competition law enforcement in which remedies can be imposed. First, remedies can be imposed in the frame of a public enforcement sanction, for example in addition to a fine. In this first situation, remedies are part of a prohibition decision, which confirms the existence of an abuse. However, remedies can also be imposed in the frame of a commitment decision. In this second situation, there is no finding of the infringement. This essay is in the framework of a commitment decision, of which, their conditions of optimality under EU competition law have been studied by Choné et al. (2004).

63. The OECD issued a report in 2022 on remedies and commitments in abuse cases and found around 30% of abuse of dominance cases with settlement or commitments in OECD countries in 2020, and around 40% for European countries[23]. The issuance of the report was fueled, among other reasons, by the growing number of enforcement actions against digital platforms. However, digital market characteristics can be specifically challenging when it comes to designing remedies. For example, the digital sector is deemed to be fast-moving and intensively innovating which can render remedies ineffective if market conditions quickly alter over time.

64. Therefore, the aim of this chapter is to study the effectiveness of remedies in the context of complex infringements in digital markets with a narrower enforcement experience.

65. Furthermore, from a sole economic risk assessment perspective, Amazon is a vertically integrated platform, with the resources to implement self-preferencing practices. If the product presented in the Buy Box is the result of a biased ranking, there is manipulation of the information provided to the consumers and a diversion of demand from potential winning sellers. This practice can be particularly damaging due to the number of consumers on Amazon's platform, with 2.7 billion visitors in July 2022.

---

22 Press release: https://ec.europa.eu/commission/presscorner/detail/en/ip_22_7777.

23 Data results from the OECD CompStata database summarised in the OECD report from 2022. In terms of total number of cases, the OECD category, accounting for 36 jurisdictions, total 24 cases abuse of dominance cases with settlement or commitment procedures in 2019, 24 cases in 2020 and 25 cases in 2021. The Europe category, accounting for 33 jurisdictions, total 20 cases abuse of dominance cases with settlement or commitment procedures in 2019, 20 cases in 2020 and 14 cases in 2021.

66. The literature in this essay relates to choice ranking, product prominence and the nascent specific literature on the competition concerns related to the Amazon's Buy Box.

67. Within the literature on the competitive risks of vertical integration, particularly in the form of product prominence and discriminatory practices, Cure et al. (2022) study the platform Kayak. The authors extracted data from Kayak's platform and observed that, for the same price, offers from online agencies affiliated to the platform are more visible than those from other agencies. The authors study the effects of vertical integration of travel agencies on the ranking of the platform's "meta-search" algorithm. To this end, they distinguish between the horizontal ranking of sales channels for the same hotel and the vertical ranking of hotels for a specific query. Their analysis identifies two risks to the optimisation of rankings by a meta-search platform in the context of vertical integration with travel agencies: the risk that hotels offered through alternative sales channels are ranked lower despite lower prices, and the risk that the ranking mechanism does not align with consumer interests.

68. Specifically, to Amazon's Buy Box, Etumnu (2022) studies the performance of third-party sellers against Amazon by distinguishing between products that are sold and shipped by Amazon, those sold by the third-party seller and shipped by Amazon (FBA: Fulfilment by Amazon) and those sold and shipped by a third-party merchant (fulfilment by Merchants). Gómez-Losada et al. (2022) studied twenty-two products on the Amazon page in Italy over a period of ten months and carried out two experiments with the aim of estimating the characteristics considered by Amazon in order for a seller to appear in the purchase box. Farronato and al. (2023) study the self-preferencing practice from Amazon with an experiment, under the angle of actual consumer searches, and find that Amazon's brands are more prominently displayed in search results.

69. Given the asymmetric information problem in the imposition of remedies—which is further exacerbated in digital markets, particularly in commitments involving modifications to opaque algorithmic rules—we aim to propose a technical solution to monitor remedies under the European Commission's decision to impose remedies on Amazon's Buy Box.

70. The closest paper to this essay is the paper from Raval (2023) which aims to study Amazon's algorithm rules to determine which seller wins the Buy Box and to measure Amazon's self-preferencing practices. Raval collected data from several countries (US, UK, Germany, France) and product categories between December 9, 2020 and January 29, 2021. In order to predict which offer wins the Buy Box, the author estimates a multinomial logit model.

71. In this essay, we first collect non-aggregated data from an Amazon price tracker. We collected data from less sub-categories than Raval (2023)

since we aimed to have at least three sellers on average over the last 90 days prior to the data collection. We also restricted our dataset in its geographic scope (ASINs sold on Amazon.fr only). We run four models: a logistical regression model, a decision tree model, a random forest model and a gradient boosting model. We obtained good to excellent prediction accuracies on the four models, from about 83% accuracy for the logit model to 94% accuracy for the gradient boosting model. Relying on machine learning technology, we created a "surrogate model" that matches the behaviour of Amazon's Buy Box and that has learned from a sample of 1,600,000 seller 1 and seller 2 pairs, which one has the best chance to win the Buy Box.

72. When we analyse the explanatory variables in our model, relying on the Shapley method, the variable *isAmazon* clearly stands out. The same result can be obtained with a logistic regression, but with a weaker predictive quality. When we tried to identify a change, relying on the hypothesis that Amazon complied with the commitments offered to the EU Commission, we can observe a change in the model around mid-2022. The 'before' model (trained on competitions before June 2022) and the 'after' model (respectively) are not identical, not interchangeable, with different qualities of precision. The values of the explanatory variables (as defined by Shapley) are not the same before and after. In particular, the price variable is more important than before and the *isAmazon* variable is less important than before. Furthermore, our descriptive analysis also shows that before mid-2022 Amazon won proportionately more competitions than after mid-2022. This leads us to believe that Amazon heavily changed its algorithm during 2022 and that it seems that a similar algorithm is at work for all the product categories observed in our sample. The change occurred gradually because the effect of the change is not sudden and is identical for all categories observed. Looking at the variables available, Amazon products have an advantage over the competition, but this advantage has significantly decreased in the course of 2022.

73. To conclude, the dissertation is articulated as follows. The first essay aims to delineate the determinants of a successful EU competition law damages action following an abuse of dominance, running a logistical regression on a dataset of 194 damages cases in France, Italy and the UK. The results are discussed against the on-going and upcoming private enforcement actions in the digital markets. The second essay aims to analyse whether Article 5 (4) of the DMA may create incentives for platforms to adapt their business model and whether business users benefit and/or also modify their own business model, with a game theory model. The third essay aims to audit the ranking strategy of the algorithm of an online platform, via data scrapping on a price tracker, after a commitment decision from the EU Commission, relying on four models, including machine learning techniques.

Chapter	Method and data	Main results
Chapter 1. Determinants of successful EU competition law damages actions following an abuse of dominance: is there anything to learn for the upcoming claims in the digital sector? Research question. What are the determinants of a successful damages action following an abuse of dominance?	• Data collected on damages actions following an abuse of dominance in France, Italy and the UK. • Original database of 194 cases. • Logistical regression analysis.	• A follow-on damages claim is less likely to be successful that a stand-alone claim. • Positive effect of the Damages Directive on the chances of success. • Introducing a claim for damages in digital markets decreases the chances of success and this effect is amplified if the claim was introduced in France.
Chapter 2. Before and after the fourth obligation of Article 5 of the DMA: business model decisions of gatekeepers and business users. Research question. Does Art 5 (4) of the DMA incentivize gatekeepers to adapt their business model and does the business user benefit and/or also modify their own business model?	• Game theory model to analyze potential changes of incentives for different business models after the introduction of a DMA obligation.	• Using the platform becomes more attractive to business users. • The anti-steering obligation is also attractive and, therefore, used by business users. To do so, they might even open their own web shop. • The platform has an incentive to become vertically integrated. • The amount of data available for business users and the platform is likely to increase. • Following the introduction of the obligation, the fees are likely to increase if already all business users were using the platform before. The effect of the obligation on the fee level is indeterminate and depends on the specific manifestation of the variables.

Chapter	Method and data	Main results
Chapter 3. Auditing the ranking strategy of a marketplace's algorithm following competition law commitments: The Amazon's Buy Box case Research question. Is it possible to audit the ranking strategy of the algorithm of an online platform, via data scrapping on a price tracker and machine learning?	• Collection of data from a third-party API for Amazon, restricted the scope to ASINs sold in France for some selected categories. • The dataset has 91,000 offers for 9,486 sellers, allowing to create 1,8 million competitions between the winning offer and every non-winning offer. • Four models: logistical regression, decision tree, random forest, and gradient boosting.	• Amazon products have an advantage over the competition, but this advantage has decreased in the course of 2022, before the commitment decision of December 2022 and even before the first set of commitments from July 2022. • Higher accuracy of the results with machine learning models.

Bibliography

Alexandrov, Alexei, George Deltas, and Daniel F. Spulber. "Antitrust and competition in two-sided markets." *Journal of Competition Law and Economics* 7, no. 4 (2011): 775-812.

Akman, Pinar. "Exploitative abuse in Article 82EC: back to basics?" *Cambridge Yearbook of European Legal Studies* 11, (2009): 9.

Andriychuk, Oles. "Do DMA obligations for gatekeepers create entitlements for business users?" *Journal of Antitrust Enforcement* 11, no. 1 (2023): 123-132.

Belleflamme, Paul and Martin Peitz. *The Economics of Platforms* Cambridge University Press, 2021.

Bougette, Patrice, Oliver Budzinski, and Frédéric Marty. "Self-preferencing and competitive damages: a focus on exploitative abuses." *The Antitrust Bulletin* 67, no. 2 (2022): 190-207.

Bougette, Patrice, Axel Gautier, and Frédéric Marty. "Business models and incentives: for an effects-based approach of self-preferencing?" *Journal of European Competition Law & Practice* 13, no. 2 (2022): 136-143.

Boyer, Marcel and Rachidi Kotchoni. "The Econometrics of Cartel Overcharges." hal-00631429 (2011).

Cabral, Luis, Justus Haucap, Geoffrey Parker, Georgios Petropoulos, Tommaso M. Valletti, and Marshall W. Van Alstyne. "The EU Digital Markets Act: A Report from a Panel of Economic Experts." *Publications Office of the European Union, Luxembourg* (2021).

Caffarra, Cristina. ""Follow the Money" – Mapping issues with digital platforms into actionable theories of harm." *e-Competitions* (2019).

Choi, Jay Pil. "Tying in two-sided markets with multi-homing." *The Journal of Industrial Economics* 58, no. 3 (2010): 607-626.

Choné, Philippe, Saïd Souam, and Arnold Vialfont. "On the optimal use of commitment decisions under European competition law." *International Review of Law and Economics* 37, (2014): 169-179.

Colangelo, Giuseppe. "DMA begins." *Journal of Antitrust Enforcement* 11, no. 1 (2023): 116-122.

Connor, John M. and Robert H. Lande. "Cartel overcharges and optimal cartel fines." *Issues in Competition Law and Policy* (2008).

Cure, Morgane, Matthias Hunold, Reinhold Kesler, Ulrich Laitenberger, and Thomas Larrieu. "Vertical integration of platforms and product prominence." *Quantitative Marketing and Economics* 20, no. 4 (2022): 353-395.

Davis, Joshua P. and Robert H. Lande. "Benefits from private antitrust enforcement: forty individual case studies." University of San Francisco Law Research Paper no. 2011-22 (2008).

Davis, Joshua P. and Robert H. Lande. "Toward an empirical and theoretical assessment of private antitrust enforcement." Seattle UL Rev. 36, (2013): 1269.

De Streel, Alexandre, Jacques Crémer, Paul Heidhues, Amelia Fletcher, Gene Kimmelman, Giorgio Monti, Rupprecht Podszun, Monika Schnitzer, and Fiona M. Scott Morton.

"The effective use of economics in the EU Digital Markets Act." *Yale Tobin Center for Economic Policy Discussion Paper* no. 8 (2023).

Decarolis, Francesco and Muxin Li. "Regulating online search in the EU: from the Android case to the Digital Markets Act and Digital Services Act." *International Journal of Industrial Organization* 90, (2023): 102983.

Etumnu, Chinonso E. "A competitive marketplace or an unfair competitor? An analysis of Amazon and its best sellers ranks." *Journal of Agricultural Economics* 73, no. 3 (2022): 924-937.

European Council. "Council Regulation (EC) No 1/2003 of 16 December 2002 on the implementation of the rules on competition laid down in Articles 81 and 82 of the Treaty (Text with EEA relevance)." OJ L 1, 4.1.2003, (2003): 1-25.

European Commission. "Communication from the Commission—Guidance on the Commission's enforcement priorities in applying Article 82 of the EC Treaty to abusive exclusionary conduct by dominant undertakings (Text with EEA relevance)." OJ C 45, (2009):7–20.

European Commission. "Commission staff working document – Impact assessment report – Damages actions for breach of the EU antitrust rules – Accompagnying the proposal for a Directive of the European Parliament and of the Council on certain rules governing actions for damages under national law infringements of the competition law provisions of the Member States and of the European union." SWD (2013) 203 final.

European Commission. "Directive 2014/104/EU of the European Parliament and of the Council of 26 November 2014 on certain rules governing actions for damages under national law for infringements of the competition law provisions of the Member States and of the European Union Text with EEA relevance." (2014) OJ L 349, 5.12.2014, p. 1–19.

European Commission, Directorate-General for Competition, Montjoye, Y., Schweitzer, H., Crémer, J., *Competition policy for the digital era*, Publications Office. (2019) https://data.europa.eu/doi/10.2763/407537

European Commission. "Impact Assessment Report, Accompanying the document: Proposal for a Regulation of the European Parliament and of the Council on contestable and fair markets in the digital sector (Digital Markets Act)." *Commission staff working document.* (2020) Part 1/2, SWD(2020) 363 final.

European Commission. "Regulation (EU) 2022/1925 of the European Parliament and of the Council of 14 September 2022 on contestable and fair markets in the digital sector and amending Directives (EU) 2019/1937 and (EU) 2020/1828 (Digital Markets Act) (Text with EEA relevance)." OJ L 265, 12.10.2022 (2022): 1–66.

Farronato, Chiara, Andrey Fradkin, and Alexander MacKay. "Self-Preferencing at Amazon: evidence from search rankings." *National Bureau of Economic Research* (2023).

Gallagher, Neil and Paulo Abecasis. "The DMA and the role of economics." *Competition Law & Policy Debate* 7, no. 3 (2022): 113-120.

Geroski, Paul A. "Competition in markets and competition for markets." *Journal of Industry, Competition and Trade* 3, (2003): 151-166.

Gómez-Losada, Álvaro, Gualberto Asencio-Cortés, and Néstor Duch-Brown. "Automatic eligibility of sellers in an online marketplace: a case study of amazon algorithm." *Information* 13, no. 2 (2022): 44.

Hotelling, Harold. "Stability in competition." *The Economic Journal* 39, no. 53 (1929): 41-57.

Janin, Lionel and Benoît Menoni. "Le contrôle des concentrations en France : une analyse empirique des avis du Conseil de la concurrence." *Economie et Prevision* 178179, no. 2 (2007): 93-114.

Jullien, Bruno and Sand-Zantman, Wilfried. "The Economics of Platforms: a theory guide for competition policy." *Information Economics and Policy* 54, (2021): 100880.

Kittaka, Yuta, Susumu Sato, and Yusuke Zennyo. "Self-Preferencing by platforms: a literature review." *Japan and the World Economy* (2023): 101191.

Komninos, Assimakis. "The Digital Markets Act: how does it compare with competition law?" *Available at SSRN 4136146* (2022).

Laborde, Jean-François. "Cartel damages actions in Europe: how Courts have assessed cartel overcharges (2021 Ed.)." *Concurrences* 03-2021, (2021): 232-242.

Lauk, Martina. "Ökonometrische Analyse Der Entscheidungspraxis Des Bundeskartellamtes." *Darmstadt Discussion Papers in Economics,*2003. https://www.econstor.eu/handle/10419/84839/.

Lin, Xiaogang, Yong-Wu Zhou, Wei Xie, Yuanguang Zhong, and Bin Cao. "Pricing and product-bundling strategies for e-commerce platforms with competition." *European Journal of Operational Research* 283, no. 3 (2020): 1026-1039.

Moreno Belloso, Natalia and Nicolas Petit. "The EU Digital Markets Act (DMA): a competition hand in a regulatory glove." *Available at SSRN 4358589* (2023).

Muthers, Johannes and Sebastian Wismer. "Why do platforms charge proportional fees? commitment and seller participation. Commitment and Seller Participation." *Review of Network Economics* 21.2 (2013): 83-110.

Newman, John M. "Antitrust in zero-price markets: applications." *Washington UL Rev.* 94, (2016): 49.

OECD. Abuse of dominance in digital markets. (2020) www.oecd.org/daf/competition/abuse-of-dominance-in-digital-markets-2020.pdf

OECD. Remedies and commitments in abuse cases, OECD Competition Policy Roundtable Background Note. (2022) www.oecd.org/daf/competition/remedies-and-commitments-in-abuse-cases- 2022.pdf

Peitz, Martin. "How to apply the self-preferencing prohibition in the DMA." *Journal of European Competition Law & Practice* 14, no. 5 (2023): 310-315.

Petit, Nicolas. "The proposed Digital Markets Act (DMA): a legal and policy review." *Journal of European Competition Law & Practice* 12, no. 7 (2021): 529-541.

Peyer, Sebastian. "Private antitrust litigation in Germany from 2005 to 2007: Empirical evidence." *Journal of Competition Law and Economics* 8, no. 2 (2012): 331-359.

Pino, Flavio. "The microeconomics of data–a survey." *Journal of Industrial and Business Economics* 49, no. 3 (2022): 635-665.

Raval, Devesh. "Steering in one click: platform self-preferencing in the Amazon Buy Box." (2023) https://deveshraval.github.io/buyBox.pdf

Rochet, Jean Charles and Jean Tirole. "Tying in two-sided markets and the honor all cards rule." *International Journal of Industrial Organization* 26, no. 6 (2008): 1333-1347.

Rochet, Jean-Charles and Tirole, Jean. "Two-sided markets: a progress report." *The Rand Journal of Economics* 37, no. 3 (2006): 645-667.

Rochet, Jean-Charles and Tirole, Jean. "Platform competition in two-sided markets." *Journal of the European Economic Association* 1, no. 4 (2003): 990-1029.

Rochet, Jean-Charles and Tirole, Jean. "Two-sided markets: an overview." *Institut d'Economie Industrielle Working Paper* (2004): 1-44.

Rodger, Barry J. "Competition law litigation in the UK Courts: a study of all cases 2005-2008-Part I." Global Competition Litigation Review (2009): 93-114.

Rodger, Barry J. "Private enforcement of competition law, the hidden story Part II: Competition litigation settlements in the UK, 2008-2012." Global Competition Litigation Review 8, no. 3 (2015): 89-108.

Segal, Ilya R. and Michael D. Whinston. "Public vs. private enforcement of antitrust law: a survey." (2006).

Sousa Ferro, Miguel. "Jurisprudência De 'Private Enforcement' (Private Enforcement Case-Law)." *Jurisprudência Portuguesa De Direito Da Concorrência Capítulo* 7, (2016).

Spulber, Daniel F. *Market Microstructure: Intermediaries and the Theory of the Firm* Cambridge University Press, 1999.

Sun, Keke. "Bundling, vertical differentiation, and platform competition." *Review of Network Economics* 17, no. 1 (2018): 1-23.

Chapter 1
Determinants of successful EU competition law damages actions following an abuse of dominance: Is there anything to learn for the upcoming claims in the digital sector?

"*It is sometimes argued that private damages actions following prosecutions by the European Commission or by national authorities could provide useful additional sanctions. The fatal problem with this argument is that, if additional monetary sanctions were indeed required, these could be provided for in a much cheaper and more reliable way by increasing the fines imposed in the public enforcement proceeding.*" Wils, 2003.

1.1 Introduction

1. This essay is an empirical study of the determinants of a successful damages action under European Union (EU) competition law provisions. The original database of damages cases covers France, Italy, and the United Kingdom (UK). In EU competition law there are more private enforcement cases following infringements to Article 101 TFEU, than for infringements to Article 102 TFEU. Therefore, this essay aims to fill in the gap in the empirical literature on damages actions for abuse of dominance position with the policy perspective of the upcoming damages actions in digital markets.

2. The Directive 2014/104/EU (Damages Directive) aims to "ensure that anyone who has suffered harm caused by an infringement of competition law by an undertaking or by an association of undertakings can effectively exercise the right to claim full compensation for that harm from that undertaking or association." (Article 1). Therefore, the EU competition law damages actions are assumed to be effective if anyone who has suffered harm caused by an infringement of competition law receives full compensation for that harm.

3. The fact that in EU competition law there are more private enforcement cases following infringements to Article 101 TFEU can be partially explained by the rebuttable presumption of harm for cartels (Art 17, Directive 2014/104/EU), which is limited to cartels "given their secret nature, which increases the information asymmetry and makes it more difficult for claimants to obtain the evidence necessary to prove the harm." (Recital 47, Directive 2014/104/EU). Hence, there is an extensive economic literature on cartels, both from a public enforcement perspective and from a private enforcement one. Administrative sanctions for infringement to Article 101 TFEU have also led to massive follow-on private enforcement. For example, following the EU Commission fining truck producers 2.93 billion euros for participating in a cartel (case AT.39824), Marcos (2023) identified 2259 Court of Appeal judgments for follow-on private enforcement on this case.

4. At the EU and national level in Member States, there has been an enforcement effort to sanction Article 102 TFEU infringements in digital markets, resulting in Big Tech firms to be heavily sanctioned. For example, Google was sanctioned for abuse of dominance by the EU Commission in the Google Shopping[1], Google Android[2], and Google Adsense[3] cases and is under scrutiny as part of the Google Adtech[4] case. Pending appeals, Google was already fined for more than 8 billion euros. However, claimants

---

1 AT. 39740.

2 AT. 40099.

3 AT. 40411.

4 AT. 40670.

in damages actions cannot rely on an extensive jurisprudence, nor on the empirical literature which extensively covers Article 101 TFEU infringements, nor on the rebuttable presumption in the Damages Directive that is limited to 101 TFEU infringements. Therefore, there is little knowledge and no empirical studies about the success of damages actions following an abuse of dominance position.

5. The research question of this essay is the following: what are the determinants of a successful damages action following an abuse of dominance?

6. The empirical study relies on an original database of damages cases following abuse of dominance infringements, in France, Italy and the United Kingdom,[5] constituted of 194 cases, from 1988 to 2023[6]. The dataset does not count decisions but cases. Therefore, each case counts from one, from the date of introduction of the complaint to the latest decision available in the observation period (until December 2022). Second, not only this research question has not yet been covered by the literature, but many economics studies on private enforcement – when not studying the quantification methodology in private enforcement cases – are papers mapping damages actions with descriptive statistics, country wide or limited to one type of infringement. Therefore, this essay allows us to study enforcement data on three EU countries with the same regulatory shock of the Damages Directive, since the Directive aims to harmonise rules between Member States for anyone who claims damages following an infringement to Article 101 or 102 TFEU.

7. While Rodger (2009 and 2015), Peyer (2012) and Sousa Ferro (2016) wrote studies covering all damages decisions for infringements to competition law restricted to one country, Laborde (2021) covered several countries but restricted his study to infringements to Article 101 TFEU. Therefore, the first originality of this essay is its database, which is not geographically restricted to only one country, but covers France, Italy and the United Kingdom. Furthermore, this essay is the first study only focusing on damages actions following abuse of dominance, as opposed to the rich literature on private enforcement following cartels infringements. The papers from Rodger (2009 and 2015), Peyer (2012), Sousa Ferro (2016) and Laborde (2021) are descriptive studies on damages actions, therefore, in terms of methods, the two empirical papers that are the closest to this essay are the papers from Lauk (2003), and Janin and Menoni (2007), which empirically study public enforcement of competition law, at the national scope, with a limited database.

---

5 The choice of including several countries in the database is first a practical choice: there are very few decisions in EU countries of damages actions for an abuse of dominance. With the notable exception of Germany, which not included both for the opposite reason and the lack of publicly available database countrywide. In his study, Peyer (2012) counted 212 cases (from 2005 to 2007) of damages actions for infringements to section 19, 20 and 21 of the ARC (Act against Restraints of Competition = Gesetz gegen Wettbewerbsbeschränkungen, GWB). Section 19 of the ARC, like Article 102 TFEU sanctions abuse of dominance. In the collection, section 19 and 20 of the ARC could not be distinguished due to lack of precise data.

6 The full list of cases considered in the study is available on request, by email to jeanne.mouton@ec.europa.eu

8. First, Lauk (2003) studied whether antitrust decisions can be explained by knowledge of the allegations and some observable market structure characteristics. The dataset is constituted of 196 antitrust and abuse cases from 1985 to 2000 in Germany. In her study, the latent variable of the probit model is the probability of a complaint by the Bundeskartellamt. The observable decision takes the value of one if the agency finds a conduct that threatens competition and zero if the conduct under investigation is found to be compliance with competition. Lauk includes market structure characteristics in the explanatory variables and a control variable to capture any intertemporal differences (influence of the acting President and the 5th amendment in 1989). The author runs several regressions, first a benchmark regression to clarify if including market structure characteristics can help improve the explanatory power of the model. Then, the inclusion of market structure variables improves the fit of the estimate. With a positive conclusion on her study, the outcome of antitrust investigations can be predicted with a relatively high rate since the Bundeskartellamt apply rules rather than making discretionary decisions.

9. Second, Janin and Menoni (2007) wrote an empirical study to understand which variables can explain the decisions of the Conseil de la concurrence in France. The dataset comprises 66 opinions from the Conseil de la concurrence, between 1988 and 2002, on merger control. Among those 66 opinions, the Conseil issues 40 favourable opinions, 17 authorisations subject to commitments and 9 non favourable opinions. In the variables set, Janin and Menoni distinguish between objective variables, that are independent of the opinions, and variables for which the Conseil has a discretionary power of appreciation. The authors also added variables of context, to either refer to the sector or to the persons in charge of instructing the case. The empirical analysis follows a two steps approach. First, the authors built descriptive statistics with the aim of describing the weight of each variable used by the Conseil to justify its opinions. Then, the authors run a logistical regression in which the explained variable is a discreet variable and can take three modalities: favourable opinion, authorisation subject to commitment and non-favourable opinion. They conclude with the observation that the variables barriers to entry, buyer power and monopole seem the key factors in the Council opinions. This result is aligned with demonstrating that the social impact of a merger is not only relying on structural factors (market shares) but also on the strategic interactions with the different market players and with the French legal texts which consider the contribution to economic progress.

10. This essay also relies on a logistical regression model.[7] The explanatory variable is the outcome of the case, which can either be positive or negative. The outcome is positive if the private parties receive compensation

7 After testing all specification under both a logistic and probit model, not significant differences were observed.

for their harm, and/or if the private parties' request for injunction is approved, or if the case closed with a settlement agreement, or if liability is established. Several hypotheses are tested.

1- A follow-on[8] case has more chance to be successful than a stand-alone case.

2- A claimant seeking injunctions as opposed to monetary damages is more likely to obtain a successful outcome on its case.

3- The introduction of the Damages Directive positively influences the success of a case.[9]

4- Claimants can expect a higher success rate depending on the sector in which there was an abuse of dominance.

Finally, in the view of the upcoming cases in the digital market,

5- A damages claim has a lower probability of success if the economic sector of the claim is the digital sector.

11. The specifications control for several factors, including, for the start year of the case, the duration of the case, as well as whether this is an individual or collective action.

12. The hypotheses of this essay are tested on an original database of damages cases following abuse of dominance infringements, in France, Italy and the United Kingdom, constituted of 194 cases, from 1988 to 2023.

13. Section I reviews the literature on the economics of litigation related to private enforcement, including the literature on antitrust damages actions following cartels infringements serving as a benchmark. Section II presents the data. Section III presents the methodology and the empirical results. Section IV discusses the results and includes an analysis of the on-going damages actions against Google following the Google Shopping case. The last section concludes the essay.

1.2 Related literature

14. When it comes to measuring the effectiveness of a law enforcement system, authors anchor their reasoning in Becker's contribution (1968) on the rationality of criminals and in Landes' (1983) when specifically measuring optimal sanctions for antitrust violations. However, each author, depending on the specificity of the law enforcement system studied, may apply different criteria, and rely on different assumptions to measure effectiveness. Therefore, there is a rich academic literature on contributions

8 A follow-on damages action follows a public enforcement sanction.

9 Two binary variables were created to test the year of the introduction of the Damages Directive (2014) and the year of the implementation of the Damages Directive (2017).

measuring either the optimal enforcement or the effectiveness of a law enforcement system.

15. The deterrence of a socially harmful behaviour can rely on two potential threats: the public enforcement of the law or the threat of private actions (Segal and Whinston, 2006). When there is combination of the possibility of public action and private enforcement, it is part of an enforcement system. Becker (1968) sets out the principle of the rationality of criminals, according to which individuals will only commit a criminal act if they derive a greater utility from it than from not committing a crime. Becker models the utility of committing a crime as follows:

$$EU = pU(b - f) + (1 - p)U(b)$$

16. Where EU is the expected utility of committing the offence, p the probability of detection and punishment, b the revenue in the event of non-detection and $(b - f)$ in the event of detection. The aim of any enforcement system is to provide incentives to comply with the law by detecting offences and punishing offenders. To achieve this deterrent effect, competition law must choose an appropriate combination of the probability of punishment and a level of fine imposed on offending firms, to provide the right incentives, i.e. minimising the difference between the utility of committing an infringement and that of not committing an infringement.

17. However, the model from Becker, setting out the rationality of criminals is a simplification of the reality. The rationality of individuals has been challenged in behavioural economics, demonstrating that individuals rely on heuristics, short-cuts, when making decisions and suffer from biases in their decision-making process (Kahneman and Tversky, 1989). The rationality of individuals is therefore bounded (Kahneman, 2003), and individuals are prone to be nudged. Back to antitrust, against the assumption of the rationality of criminals, introducing the heterogeneity of individuals (managers) engaging in cartels, Boulu-Reschef and Monnier-Schlumberger (2019) relied on an experiment to test whether some individuals, risk-taker or with an overconfidence bias, that can be qualified as hotheads[10] and be less sensitive to parameters of fine and detection in the frame of cartels. The authors find that a monetary sanction cannot deter hotheads to collude, and that there is a significative difference in the rate of choice and formation of cartels between hotheads and other participant when increasing the level of the fines. The increase in the probability of detection has also a less deterrent impact on hotheads. The existence of these individuals would be one of the reasons of persisting formation and detection of cartels despite high fines.

10 In the original French version, « têtes brulées ».

18. The debate of over versus under-enforcement of European union (EU) competition law, and therefore of the optimality and effectiveness of the fines, is a long on-going debate, which can be synthetized by the confrontation of two academic contributions. Combe & Monnier (2011) filled a gap in the existing literature with an empirical work aimed to estimate how fines should have been determined to prevent the formation of cartels. Selecting 64 cartels from 1975 to 2009, the authors compared the fine imposed with an estimation of the optimal fine (a restitution fine, amounting to the illegal profit made by the cartel). With a 100 percent of probability of detection, half of the fines amount or exceed the illegal profit, however, with 15 percent of probability of detection (a more realistic assumption), fines are below dissuasive level. Allain et al. (2011) challenge the findings of Combe & Monnier. First, the authors differentiate the objectives of restitution and deterrence with are prone to confusion. Their paper focuses on a dissuasive approach meaning that they try to set a punishment for criminal activities to be unprofitable. Using the same sample as Combe and Monnier, the authors reduce the restitutive and dissuasive benchmarks and find that two thirds of the fines are above the restitutive benchmark and half of them are above dissuasive benchmarks.

19. The legal and economic literature, in the frame of the interaction of public and private enforcement, also studied the type of fine. The EU competition damages action is characterised by a right to full compensation and is therefore opposed to the treble damages system, specific to the United States. Traditionally, public enforcement of competition law has been favoured in the EU, in contrast to the North American system, partly because of the fear of reproducing the perceived excess of treble damages litigation, which would have the effect of encouraging risk-averse defendants to settle unfounded claims (O'Donoghue, 2011). Treble damages consist of two parts: compensatory damages for the antitrust infringement and the punitive damages corresponding to the excess. In EU law, the principle of *ne bis in idem* bars the possibility of exemplary or punitive damages (Wils, 2017). Salant (1987) studies the effect of treble damages on price fixing between firms, considering the perverse effect of trebling the damage, which may encourage buyers to "damage themselves". Baker (1988) demonstrates that the dissuasive effect of antitrust damages action will depend on the extent of the private information available to cartelized firms and consumers. Besanko et Spulber (1990) build on this notion of asymmetric information. In their paper, cartelized firms have better information on production costs than their consumers and conclude that the tripling of damages is effective because of the imperfect estimation of consumers. Lande (1996) argues that compensation for antitrust damages should be higher than the actual damages and proposes adjustments to the calculation in order to consider the net cost of the violation

to third parties. He includes in his model the inefficient allocation of market power, the costs of justice and the effects of limitation periods. Segal and Whinston (2006) distinguish between the optimality of deterring treble damages in two situations, when the probability of detection is low and when the infringement is easily observable. In the second case, punitive damages would result in excessive deterrence. Finally, as Souam and Pénard (2002) point out, treble damages have also been criticised by legal experts and economists, for their inequitable redistribution of compensation and for the fact that tripling damages could dissuade companies from setting up joint ventures even though they would save costs.

20. Private enforcement is not a double sanction or solely an increase in the amount paid by the firm. Segal and Whinston (2006) study two differences between public and private action: on the one hand, the information available and the cost of acquiring it, and on the other hand, the different objectives of those who implement the law. While Polinsky and Shavell (1984) and McAfee et al. (2008) postulate that private parties have a better signal of the infringement than a public authority, Segal and Whinston (2006) limit this hypothesis according to the type of infringement of competition law. If the infringement is complex and requires knowledge of economics and market conditions, private parties lose their informational advantage in favour of public authorities and their experts. Similarly, the cost of acquiring additional information differs between public authorities and private parties. With regard to their respective objectives, private parties do not take the dissuasive effect into account when bringing their action, except in two situations: when the private parties are worried about the offender's future actions or when they have a feeling of injustice. This does not mean that an action for damages does not have a dissuasive effect, rather, that a dissuasive effect is not integrated into the choice of bringing the action. Finally, private parties are motivated by the potential financial reward of monetary damages, whereas public agencies would be motivated, in theory, by the maximisation of social well-being.

21. With regard to the interaction between public and private action, two difficulties may arise. Segal and Whinston (2006) raise the issue of screening: it is desirable for private parties to report only those actions that are socially bad but not those that are socially beneficial. McAfee et al. (2008) also point to the potentially strategic use of competition law by private parties. Finally, from a competition policy enforcement perspective, the interplay between public and private enforcement may play a role in case selection. In a speech from May 2023, Sarah Cardell, CEO of the UK Competition and Markets Authority (CMA), states that "if there is a prospect that a particular private action will overlap to a material degree with a potential public enforcement case, this will be a relevant factor in our assessment of where our resources can be put to most effective

use. For example, when deciding between which of two potential public enforcement cases to launch, if one of the cases overlaps with an existing or prospective private action, we may take that into account in our prioritisation decision, potentially leading us to launch public enforcement in the case with no overlapping private action."[11]

22. After reviewing the literature on the economics of litigation in relation to antitrust and private enforcement of antitrust, this chapter is more specifically anchored in the literature empirically studying private enforcement case law.

23. The United States (US) private antitrust action has a richer history of litigation, introduced in 1890 with the Sherman Act, then by the Clayton Act in 1914, therefore, the literature on damages actions in antitrust is richer from the US perspective. The US damages action goes beyond the action for damages in EU law because it was designed to deter anti-competitive behaviours. Another one of the major differences is that the discovery is very extensive in the US: even before any request for production of evidence is made, defendants must, by themselves, provide a certain amount of information. Class actions are also more frequent and, as proof of the adaptation of the American litigation system to these private actions, lawyers are often remunerated in the form of contingency fees, with private parties not bearing the cost of introducing the legal action. The two systems also differ on the question of indirect purchasers. In the US, the Illinois Brick rule[12] established under federal law, provides that only direct purchasers have standing to bring antitrust claims.

24. Lande and Davis wrote two studies (respectively in 2008 and 2013) aiming at an empirical assessment of US private antitrust enforcement. Their 2008 study collected data on forty of the most recent and largest cases of US private antitrust enforcement. The authors gathered data on the amount of money recovered, the proportion of the money recovered from foreign entities, whether a government action was preceding the private litigation, the amount of attorney's fees awarded to plaintiff's counsel, on whose behalf the money was recovered, and the kind of claims asserted by the plaintiff. The authors aim to compare the deterrence effect between private enforcement and federal criminal enforcement of the antitrust laws with comparing the damages recovered to the sections imposed by the Department of Justice. The authors set criteria in selecting the cases: forty recent, successful, large-scale private antitrust cases that have reached resolution and that have recovered at least $50 million. The authors also set

---

11 Speech "Private actions and public enforcement", panel remarks by Sarah Cardell, CEO of the Competition and Markets Authority, at the Competition Appeal Tribunal's 20th anniversary conference on 4 May 2023, see: https://www.gov.uk/government/speeches/private-actions-and-public-enforcement .

12 Illinois Brick Co. v. Illinois, 431 U.S. 720 (1977). This case law was at the heart of the Apple v. Pepper case (US Supreme Court, 13 May 2019, U.S. 587), in which the Supreme Court characterised mobile app purchasers "direct purchasers", hence, granting them a standing to sue in the antitrust litigation.

criteria to exclude cases: when they resulted mostly in injunctive benefits, when the cases were dismissed or unsuccessful or led to small recoveries. In their method, the authors consider as success when a plaintiff wins a favourable decision or obtains a substantial settlement. Then, they compare the amount paid in private litigation, $18.006 billion (at minimum), to the $4.232 billion paid in criminal fines. Following this, Lande and Davis conclude that private litigation provides more than four times the deterrence of the criminal fines. They also try to compare the prison sentences in the frame of the prosecutions by the Department of Justice to the amount recovered by private plaintiffs. While acknowledging that there is no objective way the deterrence effect of time spent in prison to the deterrence effect of a criminal fine, the authors rely on economics literature that attempted to value jail incarceration (Marvel et al., 1988; Dau-Schmidt et al., 1994). Lande and Davis find that half of the violations were first uncovered by private attorneys and that private litigation is more deterrent than all the fines and incarceration imposed as a result of criminal enforcement by the Department of Justice. While there are some limitations to this study (the strict selection criteria of the cases makes it difficult to generalise their conclusions), the authors conclude on the benefits of private enforcement that tend to be underreported and underappreciated.

25. From the EU perspective, there are some empirical studies of competition law damages actions, but these are either limited to one type of infringement (Article 101 TFEU) or to one country.

26. Rodger wrote two studies of UK competition law damages actions (respectively in 2009 and in 2015). Rodger starts his studies from a comparison between US and EU private enforcement where "competition law enforcement has traditionally been the virtually exclusion dominion of competition authorities", and from underlying the legislative efforts, at the EU level (taking the form of the Commission Notice on Co-operation with the National Courts in 1993 and the set of proposals) and in the UK (Competition Act 1998 and Enterprise Act of 2002), to encourage private enforcement. In the context of efforts to develop private enforcement, Rodger made a comprehensive analysis of all competition law litigation in UK Courts, involving both infringements of EC and UK competition law provisions. The author relied on the Westlaw search engine and double checked with Lexis Nexis, ending with 41 judgements identified for the period 2005-2008. Then, Rodger constructed descriptive statistics on the frequency of competition litigation, on the success rate (in his study, the success does not relate to the claim, but to the success of the competition law issue raised in the litigation, whether it is raised by the claimant or defendant), on the frequency of competition litigation, frequency of competition litigation before different Courts (First Instance Court, Appeal Court, Competition Appeal Tribunal), and on the frequency of competition follow-on action. Rodger found an increase

of the success rate in comparison to an earlier study mentioned by the author, a low rate of follow-on actions and few cases (only 8 out of 41) relying on the provisions of Article 82 or Chapter II of the Competition Act 1998 prohibiting abuse of dominance.

27. Covering Germany in his study, Peyer (2012) starts from the widely shared assumption that there is an underdevelopment of private antitrust actions at the EU level without any evidence supporting this assumption, such as a systematic data collection. Therefore, Peyer uses a dataset of private competition law decisions in Germany between 2005 and 2006, totaling 368 cases. In his case collection, faced issues with unobserved decisions, either because they were not reported or facing settlements without any public information on the content of these settlements. In his database, the author distinguishes the cases between industries in which the legal dispute took place (based on the U.K. Standard Industrial classification of Economic Activities, 2007). His database also included "other claims" which included remedies. Importantly, the prospect of success is measured by Peyer between three outcomes, "won", "partly won" or "lost". The outcome "won" occurs if the court decides in favour of the plaintiff, both with respect to the substantive pleadings and remedies request. The outcome "partly won" occurs in situation in which, for example, the judge lowers the damages awarded compared to the initial plea or grants an injunction that did not contain all the points requested. The outcome "lost" occurs when the court does not find a breach of competition law or dismisses the claim. Peyer measures, between 2005 and 2007, the frequency of private antitrust cases per year, whether claims are infringements to Article 81 and 82 EC or infringements of German provisions for unilateral conduct and horizonal and vertical anticompetitive conduct. Peyer finds that violations of EU law were only alleged in in 17.9 % of the cases (with 74.2% alleging a violation of 101 TFEU) while 74.9 % of cases alleged a violation of German law involved an accusation of unilateral conduct. This result may be explained by the fact that sections 19 and 20 of the Act against restraints of competition encompass a broader definition of unilateral behaviour than sole dominance, including the prohibition of economic dependency. Additionally, Peyer finds that the success rate differs on the type of remedy requested, with victims seeking compensation having the lowest chance of success (17.5 %), as opposed to interim relief requests. The high ratio of stand-alone cases should be interpreted, according to Peyer, as a good signal of the complementarity between public and private enforcement. However, this ratio may also reflect a lack of final public enforcement decisions. Overall, and based on the data of the study, the assumption of underdevelopment of private antitrust actions in the EU only holds true if limited to private enforcement for a violation of EU law, but if we add remedies and national provisions, plaintiffs seem active in damages actions, at least in Germany.

28. Sousa Ferro (2016) carried out a survey of competition law private enforcement cases in Portugal. Sousa Ferro identified 549 court decisions, for a total of 203 cases, from 1988 to 2016. Among the 203 cases, 88 concerned State aid, and 115 restrictive practices. The distribution of cases per year shows a trend of an increase in Court decision in private enforcement of competition law. The author also analysed the distribution of cases per Courts and judges, demonstrating the decentralized enforcement framework. Excluding from the case count one State aid dispute repeating in 107 examples, Sousa Ferro found that from 1988 to 2016 only three judges have been called upon to decide three cases of private enforcement, and no judge has decided more than three cases. The author contrasts this finding with data from the EU Commission according to which Portugal is the Member State that has given competition law trainings to the greatest number of magistrates. Furthermore, Sousa Ferro opposes the Damages Directive, that has been clearly issued with a view to follow-on damages claims from cartel infringements, with the finding that 93% of the cases of his dataset are stand-alone cases. In his paper, Sousa Ferro provides a very detailed analyses of all the cases in his dataset with selected extracts from the decisions. In relation to unilateral practices, the author identified 26 cases invoking EU or national rules on abuse of dominance.

29. Laborde builds a comprehensive review of judgments by national courts on cartel damages claims and published several editions of his study (2016, 2017, 2018, 2019, 2021). The 2016 study was built in a context of limited data to help making an informed choice on the best method to compute overcharge. At the time when the study started there was no public knowledge on which quantifications methods were accepted in cartel damages cases, neither on the frequency of the cases or in front of which courts in the EU. The 2016 study identifies 23 cases from 8 countries, out of which, only one stand-alone action, which is also the oldest case in the dataset. Laborde compares the 16%, on average, of cartel overcharge compensation, to the 20 % average cartel overcharge estimation in the EU Commission in 2009. The author interprets the lower overcharge by the nature of cases, with 19 local or national cartels, which would tend to implement lower overcharges compared to international cartels. In which case, considering the category of cartels, the numbers align with the Commission's study which estimated an average of 16% of average for national cartels. The 2017 study identifies 98 cases from 12 countries, 28 EU Member State, plus Norway and Switzerland. The method for counting cases relies on rules, among which, if large number of judgments are similar the set is regarded as a single case to avoid giving excessive weight to one cartel relatively to other cases. The study measures the damages awarded, with ranges of overcharges and reviews the methods of quantification relied upon in the cases of the dataset. In the 2018 study,

for the first time, for some countries, the list of cases was reviewed by the National Competition Authority. The 2018 study identifies 144 cases, for 242 judgements, from 13 countries, from 1988 to 2016. This study also identifies the sectors of claimants. The study provides two valuable pieces of information: experts have been appointed by courts in 28 cases and 15 damages estimations used publicly available data from the infringement decision by the National Competition Authority. In 2018, the study also emphasizes mitigation and passing-on arguments by both claimants and defendants. The 2019 study identifies 239 cartel damages actions, 59 cases in which damages were awarded, 86 cases in which liability was established and 93 cases resulting in dismissals. In Laborde's studies, a damages case is considered successful either if damages were awarded or if liability was established. Laborde observed a rapid growth of the number of cases since 52 cases were judged for the first time in 2018, compared to 24 cases judged for the first time in 2017. In the 2019 study, he also observes that out of the 59 positive overcharge estimations accepted or calculated by courts, none used regression analysis. Finally, the 2021 study covers the post Brexit EU, 27 Member States, Norway, Switzerland, and the UK, covering cases from 1988 to December 2020, and identifying 299 cartel damages actions.

30. While the previous cited studies rely on descriptive statistics, the methodology in this essay aims to test hypotheses on the determinants of success of damages claims using an econometrics model. Therefore, the methodology in this essay is closer to the following two papers. First, Lauk (2003) studies whether antitrust decisions can be explained by knowledge of the allegations and some observable market structure characteristics. The dataset is constituted of 196 antitrust and abuse cases from 1985 to 2000 in Germany. Lauk builds descriptive statistics to show the distribution of cases by categories of infringement before moving into the empirical analysis with relies on a discreet choice model. In her study, the latent variable of the probit model is the probability of a complaint by the Bundeskartellamt. The observable decision takes the value of one if the agency finds a conduct that threatens competition and zero if the conduct under investigation is found to be compliance with competition. Lauk includes market structure characteristics in the explanatory variables and a control variable to capture any intertemporal differences (influence of the acting President and the 5th amendment in 1989). To quantify the market structure, Lauk used variables such as the size distribution of companies on the supply side and whether the company concerned is the market leader. The author runs several regressions, first a benchmark regression to clarify if including market structure characteristics can help improve the explanatory power of the model. Then, the inclusion of market structure variables improves the fit of the estimate. In terms of results,

market structures features have a significant influence on the decisions of the Bundeskartellamt, both variables "market share of the largest company" as well as "market leader" are significant and have a robust influence on the decisions. The author used a control variable to capture any intertemporal differences (influence of the acting President and the 5th amendment in 1989) but there was structural break in the decisional practice. With a positive conclusion on her study, the outcome of antitrust investigations can be predicted with a relatively high rate since the Bundeskartellamt apply rules rather than making discretionary decisions. Lauk also compared her results with a study from 1999, in which Davies et al. studied the influence of market structure characteristics on decisions from the British Monopolies and Mergers Commission. While some results are similar, barriers to entry do not appear to have a significant influence on the British Monopolies and Mergers Commission. However, it was still surprising to find similarities considering the legal systems differences, German system being formalistic and rule-based and British competition policy relying on discretionary decisions. Second, Janin and Menoni (2007) wrote an empirical study to understand which variables can explain the decisions of the Conseil de la concurrence in France. The dataset comprises 66 opinions from the Conseil de la concurrence, between 1988 and 2002, on merger control. Among those 66 opinions, the Conseil issues 40 favourable opinions, 17 authorisations subject to commitments and 9 non favourable opinions. In the variables set, Janin and Menoni distinguish between objective variables, that are independent of the opinions, and variables for which the Conseil has a discretionary power of appreciation. The authors take the example of barriers to entry as potential endogenous variable: when the Conseil mention barriers to entry, it does it to justify its decision. Examples of objectives variables in their dataset are turnover condition, relevant markets, failing firm, market shares, monopoly. The authors also added variables of context, to either refer to the sector or to the persons in charge of instructing the case. Among the variables potentially endogenous: competitive assessment, buying power, barriers to entry and collusion. The empirical analysis follows a two steps approach. First, the authors built descriptive statistics with the aim of describing the weight of each variable used by the Conseil to justify its opinions.

31. Then, the authors estimate an explanatory model. To do so they run a logistical regression in which the explained variable is a discreet variable and can take three modalities: favourable opinion, authorisation subject to commitment and non-favourable opinion. For the robustness check the authors relied on the methods of jackknife and bootstrap that are better fitted to the size of their sample. They find a low precision of the results but some robustness in the model.

32. They conclude with the observation that the variables barriers to entry, buyer power and monopole seem the key factors in the Council opinions. This result is aligned with demonstrating that the social impact of a merger is not only relying on structural factors (market shares) but also on the strategic interactions with the different market players & with the French legal texts which consider the contribution to economic progress. In their limits of their study, Janin and Menoni acknowledge some potential biases in the definition of the variables, a limited number of decisions and their use of proxies.

33. In the event that someone suffered harm caused by an infringement of competition law, the first best outcome would be that private parties negotiate an economically optimal solution. This would follow the logic of private bargaining of the Coase Theorem under which if there were no transactions costs and if one of the parties owns property rights, therefore bargaining will lead to an optimal and efficient outcome. However, in the real world, there are transactions costs and even when owning transactions costs, one might not be incentivized to compensate for the damage to the property of another party. Therefore, the choice of parties to private antitrust lawsuits between settling and going to trial depends largely on the likely trial outcome and their attitudes toward risk (Perloff, Rubinfeld, Ruud; 1996). Even if transactions costs are less when a case is settled rather than tried, the attitude of parties towards risks as well as their potential strategic behaviour, might lead them to choose to trial a case rather than settle.

34. In this essay, while the first best solution would be that the introduction of a complaint by a private party leads to a settlement, we observe and measure the determinants of the second-best solution: when the Court awards for compensatory damages. This choice of observed outcome is a simplification with several flaws, among which, the potential strategic behaviour both from the defendant and from the plaintiff side is not observed. From the defendant's perspective, they have more at stake than plaintiffs because defendants are more likely to be involved in similar future litigation (Cooter & Rubinfeld, 1989). From the plaintiff's perspective, it is assumed that a damages action is only introduced if the plaintiff suffered a prejudice, that he is able to demonstrate the abuse of dominance, the causality link between his prejudice and the unilateral practice, and that he made a full evaluation of his damage. However, it is a very strong assumption, which further assumes that plaintiffs do not introduce abusive actions and have the means to demonstrate every element of their claim for damages at trial.

35. The 2004 comparative and economics study on damages reported that there were no official statistics available based upon the violation of EC competition rules in any of the Member States. The 2020 staff

working document reporting on the implementation of the Damages Directive, outlined that for a long time there was damages actions for infringements of antitrust rules were rare, therefore the first aim of the Directive is to facilitate damages actions. While the report was supposed to assess the application of the rules of the Damages Directive, it reported that sufficient operational experience has not been accumulated and did not provide official statistics of damages actions across the Member States.

36. While Rodger (2009) and 2015 Peyer (2012) and Sousa Ferro (2016) issued studies covering all damages decisions for infringements to competition law restricted to one country, Laborde (2021) covered several countries but restricted his study to infringements to Article 101 TFEU. Therefore, the first originality of this essay is its database, which is not geographically restricted to only one country, but covers France, Italy and the United Kingdom. Furthermore, if the study is restricted is restricted to infringements to Article 102, this essay is the first study only focusing on damages actions following abuse of dominance, as opposed to the rich literature on private enforcement following cartels infringements. The papers from Rodger (2009 and 2015), Peyer (2012), Sousa Ferro (2016) and Laborde (2021) are descriptive studies on damages actions, therefore, in terms of methods, the two empirical papers that are the closest in terms of methodology are the papers from Lauk (2003), and Janin and Menoni (2007). Both Lauk (2003) and Janin and Menoni (2017) rely on a probabilistic regression on a limited number of decisions and study public enforcement of competition law restricted at a national level. Among the variables of context, Janin and Menoni (2007) add the sectors as a variable, and their regression shows that some sectors a subject to a less strict merger control while other sectors, known for their anticompetitive practices, are subject to a stricter merger control. Lauk (2003) measures if there are intertemporal differences, which this essay also does, aiming to measure whether the start year of the case and whether the Damages Directive (both publication and implementation) date may positively influence the outcome of the case. Finally, Lauk (2003) compared her results with a study from 1999, in which Davies et al. studied the influence of market structure characteristics on decisions from the British Monopolies and Mergers Commission. And while some results are similar, barriers to entry do not appear to have a significant influence on the British Monopolies and Mergers Commission. However, it was still surprising to find similarities considering the legal systems differences, German system being formalistic and rule-based and British competition policy relying on discretionary decisions. Therefore, acknowledging the differences in the legal framework of damages actions in France, the United Kingdom, and Italy, this essay interacts several variables

with the country variables to observe whether the marginal effect of the variable of interest can be reinforced in a country.

37. This essay tests the following hypotheses:

- First, whether a follow-on case has more chance to be successful than a stand-alone case. This would be aligned with the fact that the Damages Directive was clearly designed to incentivize follow-on private enforcement following infringements to Article 101 TFEU.[13]
- Second, whether the type of reward sought (monetary damages or injunctions) influences the success of a case. Cauffman (2010), before the Damages Directive, identified that one of the important obstacles to the success of private enforcement of competition law is the difficulty to prove and assess the amount of damages, difficulties that she suggested could be overcome by bringing actions for injunctions instead of actions for damages. While the cases are still actions for damages, this hypothesis tests whether monetary damages or remedies asked by claimants have a positive effect on the success of a case.
- Third, whether the introduction of the Damages Directive positively influences the success of a case, which would be aligned with the goal of the Damages Directive.
- Fourth, whether claimants can expect a higher success rate depending on the sector in which there was an abuse of dominance, which could be explained by a learning effect, should a sector be more under scrutiny by private parties, the probability of success could increase with the number of cases in a specific sector.
- Finally, a damages' claim has a lower probability of success if the economic sector of the claim is the digital sector considering the complexity of infringements in digital markets.

1.3 Data

1.3.1 Original database

38. The dataset includes the latest decision issues for a private enforcement case law following an abuse of dominance in France, United Kingdom, and Italy, with a total of 194 decisions from 1988 to 2023. The gathering of the data ended in December 2022. The dataset does not count decisions but cases. Therefore, each case counts from one, from the date

13 From the 2020 staff working document reporting on the implementation of the Directive "Moreover, victims of EU competition law infringements often lodge damages actions only after a competition authority has investigated and found an infringement. They may do so, particularly to benefit from the binding effect of such finding in a follow-on damages action".

of introduction of the complaint to the latest decision available in the observation period (until December 2022).[14]

39. Data on damages actions were collected on three countries: France, United Kingdom, and Italy. In the database, there are 41 cases in France, 110 in Italy and 43 in the United Kingdom. The reasoning behind the selection of these three countries First, the decisions of private enforcement following unilateral practices were scarce in many countries. Therefore, the aim was to select at least two EU countries, since they all suffered an "external shock" with the material change in regulation, with the entry of the Damages Directive. Then, from all the EU countries, the aim was to select countries with at least twenty cases. Additionally, a practical motive led to the selection of the countries: the ability to collect as exhaustively as possible the case law. Finally, during the first phase of case identification in each country, more decisions were compiled than ultimately included in the final database, because some decisions could not be found and others were either not translatable or only partially translatable.[15]

40. Once the country scope established for this essay, it seems relevant to briefly review the legal and institutional system before the harmonization with the Directive 2014/104/EU. The deadline to transpose the Directive by the Member States was 27 December 2016 (Art 21). France transposed the Directive on the 10th of March 2017, United Kingdom on the 22nd of December 2016 and Italy on the 19th of June 2017.

Country	France	United Kingdom	Italy
Full compensation		X	
Disclosure of evidence	X		
Effect of national decisions	X	X	X
Limitation periods	X	X	X
Joint and several liability			X
Passing-on of overcharges	X		X
Quantification of harm		X	
Consensual dispute resolution		X	

Table 1: Necessary reforms for each country, per section of the Damages Directive.

41. The above table compiles for which section of the Directive 2014/104/EU, for each country in the scope of this study, some reforms were necessary. The information below was compiled from the paper of Choné-Grimaldi

14 Some latest decisions are from 2023, whenever, on a case collected until December, I noticed an update from 2023 allowing to assess the success of the case.

15 It was, for example, the case for the oldest damages cases identified in Italy.

& al. (2015). The table only refers to the national rules that were reformed with the transposition of the Directive but does not include cases when interpretation of the judges differed from the rule of law. For example, Amaro (2015) points out that the rule of full compensation is the rule of law in French civil liability, however, in some case law, the evaluation of the quantum of the damage went beyond full compensation, which could be interpreted as punitive damages.

42. The abuse of dominance is strictly understood under the EU competition law provision. The dataset includes decisions referring to an infringement to Article 86 of the Treaty of Rome (1957), to Article 82 of the European Community Treaty (2003), to Art 102 of the TFEU (2007). Therefore, the dataset excludes case law from national provisions on abuse of economic dependence (such provisions exist in France). Since the time frame is limited to the EU Treaties, it comprises decisions before and after the Damages Directive; but also, in the case of the United Kingdom, the time frame of data gathering is not limited to its withdrawal from the European Union because there were no massive reforms of antitrust private enforcement since.

43. The data collection was first initiated with the ICC Compendium of Antitrust Damages Action, which provides an overview of a selection of the most important antitrust damages case law in 21 jurisdictions. Then, and most importantly, the method for data collection was specific to each country due to the unavailability of a comprehensive publicly available record of court decisions in each country. For France, the review of the case law was first initiated with the paper from Carval and Laborde (2018) which analysed 31 cases of compensation of damages caused by an abuse of dominant position. Second, the review of the case law was completed with the papers from Amaro and al., which covered a detailed analysis of private enforcement antitrust law in France, with twelve papers, covering decisions from 2015 to June 2022.[16] Lastly, the review of the case law was completed with two legal databases: Lexis Nexis and Doctrine. For the United Kingdom, the cases from the Competition Appeal Tribunal are publicly available on its website. The case law in the UK was also reviewed with a publicly available database Bailii. For Italy, case law was gathered through the Compendium, the comprehensive ARC database[17], as well as the ITACA database.[18]

---

16 The latest paper reviewing private enforcement of antitrust law in France, at the time of the writing of this chapter, covered decisions up to June 2022, and was published in September 2022.

17 The ARC database is coordinated by the University of Trento and collects, since 1991, judgements in the field of competition, from first instance, appeal Courts and the Italian Supreme Court of Cassation.

18 Ita.ca (Italian Case-Law On Private Antitrust Enforcement) is a database which collects the decisions (final judgments; no interim orders) adopted from January 1st 2013. The project was born under the scientific and financial support of the Jean Monnet Chair "Qui a peur de l'Europe?" and was then supported by the Jean Monnet Module 'EU Specialised Judicial Protection' and by the inter-university project Comp.eu.ter, co-funded by the European Commission.

1.3.2 Description of variables

44. The data collection work started with reading all the available decisions for each case law. In the original dataset, each case amounts to an observation. Among the variables collected, some are included in the regression models, and some for descriptive statistics purposes. Several challenges were faced in constituting this database: the non-homogeneity in judgements' writing, the missing data and the non-availability of some decisions. Some variables in our dataset are observed but some are also deducted from the facts of the case. For example, in most cases the decision does not state whether the case is stand-alone or follow-on, it must be deducted from the case whether there were public enforcement proceedings sanctioning the same facts. The dataset comprises 194 decisions from 1988 to 2022. The process of data collection and their description are explained below.

Name	Description	Modelling
Success	Successful damages action	Take 1 for success
Duration	In months or days, total period between the start and end of the case	"nth_durationdays", interpreted as the effect of an additional month
Start year	Start year of the case	Continuous variable.
Follow-on	Whether it is a follow-on or stand-alone case	Take 1 for Follow-on.
Individual or collective	Whether the case is individual or collective	Take 1 for collective action.
Country	France, United Kingdom or Italy	Binary variables.
Monetary damages	Amount requested in euros	Log-linearised.
Asked remedies	Whether remedies were requested by the claimant	Take 1 when remedies were requested.
Economic Sector	Cases categories according to a list of 15 economic sectors (NACE)	Different modellings attempted.
Damages Directive	>2014 (year of entry effect)	Take 1 for every case introduced after 2014.
Transposition Directive	>2017 (end year for transposition)	Take 1 for every case introduced after 2017.

Table 2: Description of the variables.

Dependent variable

45. First, the dependent variable is the success of the case. It is a binary variable, taking 1 in case of success and zero in case of non-success. This is an observed variable, but which relies on assumptions on what is considered a successful damages action. Peyer (2012) defined three outcomes "won= if the court decided in favour of the plaintiff with respect to both the substantive pleadings and the remedy; partly won= outcomes in which, for instance, the judge lowered the amount of damages compared to the initial plea or granted an injunction that did not contain all the points requested; lost= the court did not find a breach of competition law or dismissed the claim". For Rodger (2010) the success does not relate to the claim, but to the success of the competition law issue, which can either be raised by the defendant or the claimant. In the studies from Laborde (2019), a damages action is considered successful if damages are awarded or if liability is established.[19] In this essay, there are only two outcomes, success or not success and a case is considered successful if one of the following holds: damages are awarded, remedies are imposed, a settlement was reached between parties, liability is established. The definition of a successful case in this essay might differ from what would be considered as a success by private parties. For example, if damages are awarded, even lower than the claim, the case is considered successful according to our assumptions while private parties might disagree. The opposite can also hold true. For example, private parties might introduce a claim for damages, to signal the infringement on the market, with the aim of reaching a settlement outside Court. In the event of discontinuance of proceedings, the outcome is considered successful only if information was gathered on a settlement reached. However, there is no public record on private settlements. In some cases, it is mentioned that the case was closed due to a settlement, but we expect that more settlements will be reached than there is information available on this subject.

46. Among the 194 cases, 109 resulted in a successful outcome (=1 for the variable "success", and 85 were not successful.

Follow-on and stand-alone cases

47. The cases have been categorised between follow-on and stand-alone cases. A follow-on damages action follows a public enforcement proceeding at the national or EU level. A stand-alone proceeding occurs when private parties cannot rely on a public enforcement decision,

19 The event that outcome of the case is positive if the liability is established as a criterion is used for on-going cases, whenever the case is not over yet (for example, the quantum of damages not yet defined), but the Court already established the liability of the defendant.

and therefore, also must demonstrate the anticompetitive practice. If damages actions follow a commitment procedure, it is classified as stand-alone case in this essay, since there is no formal decision sanctioning the anticompetitive practice.

48. In this database, 69 cases were follow-on, and 125 cases were stand-on cases. This trend differs from what was observed in damages studies following cartels infringements, in which follow-on damages cases prevail (Laborde, 2021).

Time period scope

49. There are several dates variables: start date, end date, start year, end year and duration of the case. The aim was to collect the date of the introduction of the claim and the date of the final decision. If the decision did not indicate the date of the introduction of the claim, then the date of the pre-decision hearing or first instance decision was included instead. When the case is still on-going the latest decision or latest order of the Chair or latest case management hearing date was included. There is also a variable date *Damages Directive*, which takes one for cases introduced after 2014.

50. The graph below shows that there are very few cases in before 2000. The 50% percentile of the cases distribution is in 2013, and the 75% percentile in 2015, the mean being in 2011.

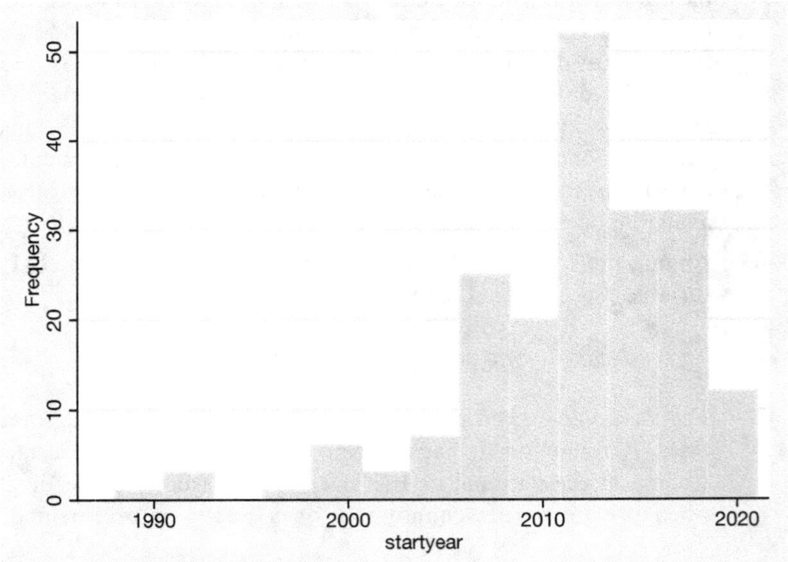

Figure 1: Distribution of the cases per start year.

Geographic scope

51. Each case is also classified according to the country in which the legal action was initiated: France, United Kingdom, or Italy. In the database, there are 41 cases in France, 110 in Italy and 43 in the United Kingdom. The below table summarizes, per country, what is the minimum, maximum, mean start year and duration in days of a case:

Country	Start Year	Duration in days	
France	1988	10	*Min*
	2009.561	2109.073	*Mean*
	2012	1772	*P50*
	2020	9276	*Max*
Italy	1993	7	*Min*
	2012.627	1829	*Mean*
	2013	1787	*P50*
	2020	5301	*Max*
United Kindgom	1997	10	*Min*
	2011.023	710.814	*Mean*
	2011	403	*P50*
	2021	4301	*Max*

Table 4: Start Year and Duration of cases per country.

52. The oldest case in the database was initiated in France. In terms of duration of the cases, the shortest mean is attributed to cases in the United Kingdom, compared to the highest mean of 2109,073 days for cases initiated in France. The 2020 staff working document reporting on the implementation of the Damages Directive, quoting several studies on damages claims following a cartel infringement, notes that in follow-on actions following a cartel, it takes approximately 13 years between the purchase of the product or service subject to a public enforcement decision and the first civil judgment.

53. The table below summarises, per country, the minimum, average, 50th percentile and maximum amount in euros of monetary damages requested and obtained:

Country	Asked Damages	Granted Damages	
France	0	0	*Min*
	6.07e+07	7453470	*Mean*
	3610533	36695	*P50*

Country	Asked Damages	Granted Damages	
	5.78e+08	1.82e+08	*Max*
Italy	0	0	*Min*
	5.64e+07	315094.4	*Mean*
	1039680	0	*P50*
	3.28e+09	8377084	*Max*
United-Kingdom	0	0	*Min*
	7.70e+10	443337.6	*Mean*
	72067.53	0	*P50*
	1.00e+12	3874077	*Max*

Table 5: Monetary damages requested by country.

54. The table clearly shows the gap between the amount of damages requested in Court and granted. In Italy and in the United Kingdom the 50th percentile of the amount of damages requested is at 0. When computing the difference, in percentage, between the amount of damages requested and granted, the average is at 0,12 in France, 0,22 in Italy and 0,08 in the United Kingdom.

55. Furthermore, remedies were requested in 8 cases in France, 61 cases in Italy and 23 cases in the United Kingdom. Remedies were granted in 7 cases in France, 22 cases in Italy and 9 cases in the United Kingdom.

Individual vs. collective actions

56. The cases were categorised between individual versus collective action. A collective action, or class action, allows several individuals who suffered the same damage, to gather their claims. There is no provision for a harmonized class actions under the Damages Directive, therefore, it differs from each national legal provisions. In Italy, collective actions following infringement to competition law are possible since December 2007[20], since 2014 in France[21] and since 2015 in the United Kingdom.[22]

Economic sector

57. Each case is classified by economic sector. The economic sectors were deducted from the relevant market in the decision, from the list of NACE code. For the purpose of comparing economic sectors, the cases are classified according to the first letter of the NACE code, which can be a

20 Article 140-bis of the Italian Consumer Code ("Article 140-bis"), enacted as Article 2, paragraph 446, of Italian Law 12.24.2007 No. 244 (the "Financial Act").

21 France, Class actions were introduced in France by Law No. 2014-344 of 17 March 2014 and have been actionable since October 2014. This Law only enabled class actions related to consumer and competition law breaches.

22 Consumer Rights Act, 1 October 2015, amending Competition Act 1998.

broad economic sector, for example, letter "J" regroups information and telecommunications, which also includes data processing and web portals. The below table shows the frequency of cases per economic sector. Three economic sectors stand up with a higher frequency of cases: information and communication, manufacturing and transporting and storage.

Economic sector name	Freq.	Percent
Accommodation and food service activities	1	0.52
Advertising and market research	3	1.55
Arts, entertainment and recreation	5	2.58
Construction	1	0.52
Electricity, gas, steam and air conditioning supply	10	5.15
Financial and insurance activities	4	2.06
Information and communication	59	30.41
Manufacturing	26	13.40
Mining and quarrying	2	1.03
Motion picture, video and television programme production, sound recording and music publishing activities	2	1.03
Pharmaceutical products	10	5.15
Publishing activities	9	4.64
Transporting and storage	54	27.84
Water supply; sewerage; waste management and remediation activities	3	1.55
Wholesale and retail trade	5	2.58
Total	194	100.00

Table 3: Frequency of cases per economic sector.

Monetary damages versus remedies

58. Whenever available, the dataset comprises the amount of the damages claimed (in first instance) and the amount of the damages awarded. All amounts have been converted to euros (pounds and francs). Several biases may arise in collecting these data. First, in the UK, the quantum is often only discussed later in the procedure, once the claim for damages is cleared.[23] The collection of data on the quantum of damages claimed and awarded can suffer from several limits. First, in some cases, the legal interests were

23 For example, in the UK Competition Appeal Tribunal, Socrates Training Limited v The Law Society of England and Wales, 26 May 2017: "By order of 16 May 2016, the Tribunal directed that the issue of liability should be determined separately and in advance of any question of the quantum of Socrates' damages in the event that it succeeds in its claim."

expressly included in the calculation of the damages awarded, in some others, it is unclear. In French cases, the amount for the reimbursement of procedural costs (Article 700 civil procedure code) was deducted from the damages awarded, since it was not possible to collect this data on most cases. In two French cases, the final sum of damages awarded required to consider the specificity of the procedure.[24] Two separates, binary variables, were also included whenever remedies were requested and awarded.

59. Among the 194 cases of the dataset, monetary damages were requested by the claimants in 127 cases. The mean of the value of monetary damages greatly differs from the 50th percentile, indicating that the data are skewed. Claimants also requested remedies in 92 cases and remedies were granted in 38 cases.

1.4 Empirical analysis

60. The empirical analysis in this chapter aims to understand the variables determining successful EU competition law private enforcement. The regression is a logistical model, in which the dependent variable is the outcome of the case. It is a binary variable since there are only two outcomes, success or not success and a case is considered successful if one of the following holds: damages are awarded, remedies are imposed, a settlement was reached between parties, or liability is established.

61. Several specifications of the regression are run to test the following hypothesis.

62. *First hypothesis:* A follow-on damages claim is more likely to be successful that stand-alone claim since they follow a public enforcement decision in which the dominance of the defendant has been established, lowering the burden of proof on the plaintiff.

63. The logistic regression is specified as follows:

$$Y_{success} = \beta_{constant} + \beta_1 X_{followorstandalone} + \beta_2 X_{duration} + \beta_3 X_{startyear} + \beta_4 X_{collectiveactions} + \varepsilon$$

64. Where, Y is the outcome of the case proceedings, which takes 0 for negative and 1 for positive, X_1 is a binary variable taking 1 for a follow-on and 0 for a stand-alone action, X_2 is a continuous variable on the duration of the case, X_3 is the start year of the case, X_4 is a binary variable taking 0 is the action is individual or 1 if the action is collective. An error term is also added.

24 In the decision Tribunal de commerce, SA Dufry France c/ SNC Relay France, 27/09/2011, the judge expressly deducted a transaction from the final damages awarded, however the amount of the transaction was not disclosed. In the decision Cour d'appel de Paris, SARL P. Streiff Motorsport et al. c/ SAS Speedy, 28/06/2022, the judge deducted the free participation to the 2000 edition of the competition (sponsorship fee), but the fee amount was not disclosed, so the repair in kind was added to the overall damages awarded in the dataset for this case.

Dep. Variable:		**Success**	
	(1)	**(2)**	**(3)**
Follow On	−0.944***	−1.484***	0.481
	(−2.87)	(−3.98)	(0.97)
Duration	0.00471	0.00233	0.00034
	(1.17)	(0.50)	(0.08)
Start Year	0.0626*	0.0519	0.0441
	(2.18)	(1.74)	(1.43)
Collective actions	−2.057*	−2.044*	−1.845*
	(−2.53)	(−2.45)	(−2.20)
United-Kingdom		−1.161*	
		(−2.42)	
Follow On x United-Kingdom		2.844**	
		(3.25)	
Italy			1.363**
			(3.18)
Follow On x Italy			−2.524***
			(−3.75)
Constant	−125.4*		
	(−2.17)		
N	194	194	194
R^2	0,785	0,1253	0,1378

T-Statistics in parenthesis
*** p<0.05, ** p<0.01, *** p<0.001**
Coefficients are estimated by a logistic estimation.

65. The first model, (1) success, is the baseline model of the specification. The variable *Follow-on* is statistically significant, with a negative coefficient, therefore, in the baseline model, the probability of success of a follow-on case to lead to a successful outcome decreases by comparing to a stand-alone case. The second model, (2) success, introduces an interaction with the country variable *United-Kingdom* and the *Follow-on* situation, the two variables interacted are statistically significant, but this time the total marginal effect of *Follow-on* become positive. Therefore, the probably of success in the event of a follow-on case is largely amplifies if it happens in the *United-Kingdom*. The third model, (3) success, introduces an interaction between *Follow-on* and the country variable *Italy*. The third model has the highest R-squared (0,1378 opposed to the 0,785 of the baseline model). In this model, the variable *Follow-on* is not by itself statistically significant, but its interaction with the variable Italy is statistically significant, with a negative coefficient, contrary to the interaction with the country variable *United-Kingdom*.

66. *Second hypothesis:* A claimant seeking injunctions as opposed to than monetary damages is more likely to obtain a successful outcome on its case.

67. The logistic regression is specified as follows:

$$Y_{success} = \beta_{constant} + \beta_1 X_{followorstandalone} + \beta_2 X_{duration} + \beta_3 X_{startyear} + \beta_4 X_{collectiveactions} + \beta_5 X_{remediesrequest} + \beta_6 X_{monetarydamagesrequest} + \varepsilon$$

68. Where, Y is the outcome of the case proceedings, which takes 0 for negative and 1 for positive, X_1 is a binary variable taking 1 for a follow-on and 0 for a stand-alone action, X_2 is a continuous variable on the duration of the case, X_3 is the start year of the case, X_4 is a binary variable taking 0 is the action is individual or 1 if the action is collective, X_5 is a binary variable taking 0 where remedies were requested and 1 when they were not, X_6 is a continuous variable measuring the monetary damages requested. The collect of the variable "monetary damages" was also attempted as a binary variable but was not satisfactory. An error term is also added.

Dep. Variable:	**Success**
	(1)
Follow-on	−1.229**
	(−3.05)
Duration	−0.00167
	(−0.29)
Start Year	−0.00546
	(−0.12)
Collective actions	0
	(.)
Asked Damages	0.107
	(1.54)
Asked Remedies	0.0704
	(0.17)
Constant	10.47
	(0.11)
N	120
R^2	0.0718

T-Statistics in parenthesis
*** p<0.05, ** p<0.01, *** p<0.001**
Coefficients are estimated by a logistic estimation.

69. Several modellings of the specification were attempted, including log-linearisation and non-linear link transforming the variable *Asked Damages*, controlling for a country effect and replacing the variable *Start Year* by *Directive Damages* and *Tranposition Directive*. The variable *individual actions* was dropped. The variables *Asked Damages* and *Asked remedies* are not statistically significant in all the models. Therefore, we fail to reject the null hypothesis.

70. *Third hypothesis:* The date of promulgation of the Directive as well as the date of the implementation of the Directive should positively influences the success of damages cases, in alignment with the goal of the Damages Directive.

71. The logistic regression is specified as follows:

$$Y_{success} = \beta_{constant} + \beta_1 X_{followorstandalone} + \beta_2 X_{duration} + \beta_3 X_{collectiveactions} + \beta_4 X_{damagesdirective} + \varepsilon$$

72. Where, Y is the outcome of the case proceedings, which takes 0 for negative and 1 for positive, X_1 is a binary variable taking 1 for a follow-on and 0 for a stand-alone action, X_2 is a continuous variable on the duration of the case, X_3 is a binary variable taking 0 is the action is individual or 1 if the action is collective, X_4 is a binary variable taking 1 if the year of the case is after 2014 to measure the effect of the entry of the Damages Directive. The X_4 binary variable is also modelled to measure the effect of the transposition of the Damages Directive, taking 1 if the year of the case is after 2016. An error term is also added.

Dep. Variable:	**Success**	
	(1)	**(2)**
Duration	0.00368	0.00448
	(0.95)	(1.13)
Follow-on	−0.900**	−0.857**
	(−2.75)	(−2.60)
Collective actions	−1.991*	−2.272**
	(−2.46)	(−2.64)
Damages Directive	0.647*	
	(1.99)	
Transposition Directive		1.325**
		(2.63)
Constant	0.236	0.241
	(0.78)	(0.85)

Dep. Variable:	Success	
N	194	194
R^2	0.0753	0.0906

T-Statistics in parenthesis
*** p<0.05, ** p<0.01, *** p<0.001**
Coefficients are estimated by a logistic estimation.

73. Both variables *Damages Directive* and *Transposition Directive* are statistically significant, with a positive coefficient, indicating that the probability of the outcome of the case to be a success being greater since the entry of the Damages Directive by 0,647 points of percentage, and even greater since 2017, date to transpose the Directive, by 1,325 points of percentage.

74. *Fourth hypothesis:* The chance of success depends on the economic sector of the defendant's undertaking in which the claim was introduced. If the claim is introduced in an economic sector in which there were already several cases damages cases, then the chances of success are higher.

$$Y_{success} = \beta_{constant} + \beta_1 X_{followorstandalone} + \beta_2 X_{duration} + \beta_3 X_{startyear} + \beta_4 X_{ecosector} + \beta_5 X_{monetarydamagesrequest} + \varepsilon$$

75. Where, Y is the outcome of the case proceedings, which takes 0 for negative and 1 for positive, X_1 is a binary variable taking 1 for a follow-on and 0 for a stand-alone action, X_2 is a continuous variable on the duration of the case, X_3 is the start year of the case, X_4 is a continuous variable indicating the number of cases per economic sector, X_5 is a continuous variable measuring the monetary damages requested. An error term is also added.

76. Several modellings of the variable *Economic Sector* were attempted. The first modelling attempted included the 15 economic sectors of the dataset, the second one categorises the economic sectors in three groups (two groups with the economics sectors with more than fifty cases against the rest).

Dep. Variable:	Success	
	(1)	**(2)**
Start Year	0.0653	–0.00457
	(1.93)	(–0.09)
Duration	0.00524	0.000615
	(1.09)	(0.10)
Collective actions	–1.908*	0
	(–2.17)	(.)
Follow-on	–0.855*	–0.938*
	(–2.30)	(–2.18)

Dep. Variable:	Success	
	(1)	(2)
Advertising and market research	0	
	(.)	
Arts, entertainment & recreation	−0.496	
	(−0.32)	
Construction	0	
	(.)	
Electricity, gas, steam and air conditioning supply	0.786	
	(0.51)	
Financial and Insurance activities	1.920	
	(1.04)	
Information and communication	0.223	
	(0.17)	
Manufacturing	0.754	
	(0.56)	
Mining and quarrying	0	
	(.)	
Motion picture, video and television programme production, sound recording and music publishing activities	1.081	
	(0.55)	
Pharmaceutical products	0.615	
	(0.43)	
Publishing activities	0	
	(.)	
Transporting and storage	−0.101	
	(−0.08)	
Water supply; sewerage; waste management & remediation activities	0	
	(.)	
Wholesale and retail trade	0	
	(.)	
Accommodation and food service activities	0	
	(.)	
France	−0.0366	−0.986

Dep. Variable:	**Success**	
	(1)	**(2)**
	(−0.06)	(−0.94)
Italy	0.567	−0.299
	(1.21)	(−0.29)
Sectors other than information and communication or transports		0
		(.)
Information and communication		−1.211*
		(−2.24)
Transporting and storage		−1.321*
		(−2.26)
Asked Damages		0.124
		(1.50)
Constant	−131.6	9.491
	(−1.93)	(0.10)
N	174	120
R^2	0.1134	0.1215

T-Statistics in parenthesis
*** p<0.05, ** p<0.01, *** p<0.001**
Coefficients are estimated by a logistic estimation.

77. The variable *Economic Sector* was sub-categorised for each economic sector, some were dropped, and none are significant. However, the sectors Information and communication Transports are statistically significant. Therefore, introducing a claim in those sectors decreases the probably of success compared to the others sectors (as a whole) from this database.

78. The modelling of variable *Number decisions* kept in the regression indicates the number of cases per economic sector. This modelling aims to measure the effect of the economic sector as a learning effect, if a greater number of cases in an economic sector may lead to a greater probability of success.

Dep. Variable:	**Success**		
	(1)	**(2)**	**(3)**
Start Year	0.0670*	−0.0332	−0.0311
	(2.30)	(−0.66)	(−0.63)
Duration	0.00536	−0.000725	−0.000187
	(1.33)	(−0.12)	(−0.03)
Collective actions	−2.055*	0	0

Dep. Variable:		Success	
	(1)	(2)	(3)
	(−2.53)	(.)	(.)
Follow-on	−0.877**	−0.849*	−0.947*
	(−2.64)	(−1.98)	(−2.17)
Number Decisions	−0.0101	0.00670	−0.0741**
	(−1.42)	(0.50)	(−3.03)
Italy		4.119**	
		(2.76)	
Italy x Number Decisions		−0.0817**	
		(−2.87)	
Asked Damages		0.128	0.120
		(1.57)	(1.55)
France			−4.318**
			(−3.00)
France x Number Decisions			0.0870**
			(3.10)
Constant	−134.0*	65.39	65.38
	(−2.29)	(0.65)	(0.66)
N	194	120	120
R^2	0.0861	0.1765	0.1928

T-Statistics in parenthesis
*** p<0.05, ** p<0.01, *** p<0.001**
Coefficients are estimated by a logistic estimation.

79. In the first, (1) success, baseline model, the variable *Number Decisions* is not statistically significant. Then, two models were attempted, with an interaction with the country variables. For both models, the variable *Individual actions* was removed since it was dropped from a regression, predicting failure perfectly. Furthermore, the variable *Asked Damages* was added, as it improved the fit of the R-square. The second model, (2) success, shows that the interaction between *Italy* and *Number Decisions* is statistically significant, meaning that the probability of success decreases with the number of decisions in an economic sector. The third model, (3) success, shows that that the interaction between *France* and *Number Decisions* is statistically significant, meaning that the probability of success increases with the number of decisions in an economic sector. The third model has the best fitted with the higher R-square (0,1928, against 0,1765 for the second one and 0,0861 for the first one). The interaction between *United-Kingdom* and *Number Decisions* is not figured in the table above as it was not statistically significant.

80. *Fifth hypothesis:* A damages claim has a lower probability of success if the economic sector of the claim is the digital sector.

$$Y_{success} = \beta_{constant} + \beta_1 X_{followorstandalone} + \beta_2 X_{duration} + \beta_3 X_{startyear} + \beta_4 X_{Digitalsector} + \beta_5 X_{monetarydamagesrequest} + \varepsilon$$

81. Where, Y is the outcome of the case proceedings, which takes 0 for negative and 1 for positive, X_1 is a binary variable taking 1 for a follow-on and 0 for a stand-alone action, X_2 is a continuous variable on the duration of the case, X_3 is the start year of the case, X_4 is a continuous variable indicating the number of cases per economic sector, X_5 is a continuous variable on the amount of asked damages log transformed. An error term is also added.

Dep. Variable:		**Success**	
	(1)	**(2)**	**(3)**
Start Year	−0.0295	−0.0218	−0.0346
	(−0.55)	(−0.44)	(−0.65)
Duration	−0.00252	−0.000837	−0.00252
	(−0.37)	(−0.14)	(−0.40)
Collective actions	0	0	0
	(.)	(.)	(.)
Follow-on	−1.527***	−1.354**	−1.362**
	(−3.46)	(−3.21)	(−3.20)
Asked Damages	0.0382	0.154	0.168*
	(0.42)	(1.93)	(2.04)
Digital Sector	−8.364**	−1.334*	0.482
	(−2.64)	(−2.30)	(0.66)
Digital Sector x Asked Damages	0.485*		
	(2.47)		
France	−0.657		
	(−0.62)		
Italy	−0.254		
	(−0.24)		
France		−0.960	
		(−1.63)	
Digital Sector x France		1.787	
		(1.92)	
Italy			0.989

Dep. Variable:		Success	
	(1)	(2)	(3)
			(1.66)
Digital Sector x Italy			−2.026*
			(−2.19)
Constant	60.65	43.17	68.06
	(0.56)	(0.43)	(0.64)
N	120	120	120
R^2	0.1321	0.1124	0.1188

T-Statistics in parenthesis
*** p<0.05, ** p<0.01, *** p<0.001**
Coefficients are estimated by a logistic estimation.

82. The variable *Individual actions* was dropped (predicted perfectly) and the variable *Asked Damages* was added to improve the fit of the model. In the baseline line model, (1) success, the variable *Digital sector* is statistically significant with a negative coefficient, however, when interacted with the variable *Asked Damages* the interaction is statistically significant with a positive coefficient. In the second model, (2) success, the variable *Digital sector* is interacted with the country variable *France*, the variable *Digital sector* is statistically significant with a negative coefficient. In the third model, the variable *Digital sector* is not statistically significant with a positive coefficient, but the interaction of the variable *Digital sector* with the country variable *Italy* is statistically significant with a negative coefficient.

83. The below table summarises the results for each hypothesis:

Hypothesis	Variables and coefficients	Result
A follow-on damages claim is more likely to be successful that stand-alone claim.	Negative and statistically significant coefficient of the variable *Follow-on*.	Fail to reject the null hypothesis.
A claimant seeking injunctions as opposed to than monetary damages is more likely to obtain a successful outcome on its case.	The variables *Asked Damages* and *Asked remedies* are not statistically significant in all the models.	Fail to reject the null hypothesis.
The date of promulgation of the Directive as well as the date of the implementation of the Directive should positively influences the success of damages cases	Both variables *Damages Directive* and *Transposition Directive* are statistically significant, with a positive coefficient.	Reject the null hypothesis.

Hypothesis	Variables and coefficients	Result
The chance of success depends on the economic sector of the defendant's undertaking in which the claim was introduced.	Sectors variables *Information and communication Transports* are statistically significant.	Fail to reject the null hypothesis for all economic sectors.
In the view of the upcoming cases in the digital market, we test whether damages claims have a higher probability of success if the economic sector of the claim is the digital sector.	*Digital sector* is statistically significant with a negative coefficient in the baseline model, effect amplified if the claim is introduced France.	Reject the null hypothesis.

Table 6: Summarising the results from the empirical analysis.

1.5 Discussion and policy recommendations

84. While there is an extensive legal and procedural literature questioning the effectiveness of private enforcement of competition law in the EU as well as the shortages of the Damages Directive, the empirical literature outside the quantification methods for damages actions following Article 101 TFEU infringements is limited. Therefore, this essay aims to fill in the gap in the empirical literature on damages actions for abuse of dominance position with the policy perspective of the upcoming damages actions in digital markets.

85. The results of the empirical analysis can be summarized as follows. Using a logit specification, the estimates identify correlations rather than causal effects. The first hypothesis examined whether follow-on cases are associated with a higher likelihood of success compared to standalone cases, which would be consistent with the Damages Directive's objective of incentivizing follow-on private enforcement of Article 101 TFEU. The estimates indicate that follow-on damages cases are, on average, associated with a lower probability of success, an association that is more pronounced in the United Kingdom. The second hypothesis explored whether the type of relief sought, monetary damages or injunctive remedies, is related to case outcomes. The regression results indicate that neither the amount of damages claimed nor the request for non-monetary remedies is statistically associated with the probability of a successful outcome. The third hypothesis examined whether the timing of the introduction of the Damages Directive is associated with case success, in line with the Directive's stated objectives. The results suggest that both the entry year and the transposition year of the Damages Directive are positively and statistically associated with

successful outcomes. The fourth hypothesis investigated whether case outcomes are correlated with the defendant's economic sector. When considering sectoral differences, cases in the information and communication sector and in the transportation sector are associated with a lower probability of success. In addition, when using the number of cases within a given sector as a proxy for a potential learning effect, the estimated association differs across jurisdictions: the probability of success is positively associated with sectoral case concentration in France, but negatively associated in Italy. Finally, given the growing importance of digital markets, the fifth hypothesis examined whether cases brought in the digital sector are associated with different outcomes. In the baseline model, claims in the digital sector are associated with a lower probability of success, an effect that is more pronounced in Italy. However, when interacting the digital sector variable with the log-linearized amount of damages, the interaction term is positive and statistically significant, suggesting that the relationship between digital-sector cases and success may vary with the scale of the claim.

86. While it may be surprising that follow-on cases are less likely to be successful than stand-alone cases, it seems to indicate a clear difference in litigation of damages actions between infringements to Article 101 and 102 TFEU. First, in this database, 69 cases were follow-on, and 129 cases were stand-alone cases. There is almost one follow-on case for two stand-alone cases. If we compare this descriptive statistic with Laborde latest study (2021) assessing overcharge on cartel infringements, this trend largely differs in his database, since Laborde finds that over the 299 cases of his database,[25] 57% followed an infringement decision made by a national competition authority, 40% followed a European Commission decision, and only 2% were stand-alone actions. One interpretation of this essay's results that follow-on damages cases have less chances of success, in the context of greater number of stand-alone cases following Article 102 TFEU infringements, could be that claimants do not benefit from the presumption set up in Article 17 of the Damages Directive that cartels cause harm. Therefore, while claimants for damages following an Article 102 TFEU infringement still benefit from Article 9 of the Damages Directive, on the effect of public enforcement decisions, their expected utility in waiting years for a public enforcement case to be litigated is lower, compared to claimants for damages following an Article 101 TFEU. This effect is amplified by first the fact that more cartel cases are litigated than abuse of dominance, with cartels cases accounting for the majority of the fines.[26] This effect could be further amplified if

25 From 1998 to 2020, covering 27 Member States plus Norway, Switzerland and the United Kingdom.

26 Data from the OECD Competition Trends 2023, available at: OECD Competition Trends 2023 | OECD iLibrary (oecd-ilibrary.org) (last accessed on 11/05/2024).

abuse of dominance cases takes longer to be litigated, but there are no available comparative studies on the duration of antitrust cases. In any case, litigation experience has shown that abuse of dominance cases takes longer to be litigated in digital sector.[27]

87. The results suggest that the choice between claiming monetary damages and requesting remedies is not statistically associated with the outcome of the claim. Cauffman (2010) requesting injunctions could overcome the difficulty in quantifying damages. Further, one could argue that requesting remedies could send a signal from the claimant to the judge that it is less likely that the claim is frivolous or malicious. However, in most cases, when asking remedies, the claimant was also requesting monetary damages. In 92 cases in which remedies were requested, monetary damages were also requested in 57 cases.[28] Therefore, there does not seem to be a clear-cut exclusive strategy from the claimants, between requesting monetary damages or requesting remedies.

88. The positive and statistically significant associations observed for both the Damages Directive and its transposition are not unexpected and are consistent with the Directive's objective of harmonising rules across Member States for parties seeking damages for infringements of Articles 101 and 102 TFEU. However, a longer time horizon and additional observations would be required to assess the magnitude of these associations more precisely and to evaluate whether the Directive is associated with increased incentives to bring damages claims. Indeed, since the Damages Directive there have been several requests for preliminary rulings, some are still on-going, and additional years of crystallisation of these rulings could increase incentives for the claimants. To only quote one example of a key preliminary ruling, in the Cogeco case,[29] Sport TV was sanctioned by the Portuguese Competition Authority for abuse of a dominant position on the market for the broadcasting of 'premium' sports television channels. Gogeco, a pay-TV provider, harmed by the excessive pricing of Sport TV, introduced a claim for damages. The national court referred to the EU Court of Justice to clarify the temporal scope of the Damages Directive, which specified both when the Directive should take effect and clarified the conformity of national law provisions relating to the limitation period of actions for damages brought prior to the transposition of the directive (Bernardeau, 2019).

---

27 From the Commission Staff working document impact assessment report accompanying the proposal regulation DMA, §119: "*As a recent report by the European Court of Auditors ('ECA') also indicates "particularly in the digital economy, this may be too late to tackle a competition problem". (...) Moreover, – even when using interim measures, explained below – competition law enforcement requires a detailed economic and legal analysis which, jointly with the procedural safeguards, bring the duration of the investigations to at least around two years and usually more than that.*"

28 In twelve cases, there is clear information that claimants did not ask for monetary damages and in 23 cases it was not possible to assert whether monetary damages were also claimed.

29 C-637/17 – Cogeco Communications.

89. The negative association observed for the transport and storage sector can be further explored by examining the underlying cases in greater detail. There are 54 cases in the transports and storage economic sector, among which, 43 cases in Italy, in which 17 private enforcement cases were follow-on cases on the A377 decision from the AGCM. While those were mainly successful, the two main reasons why private enforcement cases failed in Italy were because the claimant could not bring the lack of evidence or because of the five-year prescription. The remainder of the cases in the transports and storage economic sector were mostly litigated in the UK (9 cases), where in most occurrences claims were dismissed or withdrawn, where in one case abuse of dominance was not established and in one case causation caused issue as well as the certification of the case due to the variable characteristics of the claimants (collective action). In the transports sector, there were two French cases, one succeeded, recovering 4% of the amount of monetary damages claimed and in the other one the Court decided that the claimants did not prove the practice of low price invoked, which would have required to be enough spread and permanent. Regarding the negative effect of the information and communication sector[30], which also corresponds to the Digital sector in the last model, there are 59 cases in the dataset which are distributed as follows, 30 cases in Italy, 15 cases in France and 14 cases in the UK. In Italy, most of the cases in this sector failed, the main reasons being the lack of evidence, either of abuse of dominance or of damage, and the prescription. In France, while most cases were successful, they collected, on average, 11% of the amount of the monetary damages requested. In the UK, one claim was withdrawn, two cases fail because the abuse of dominance could not be established, and one case failed because the Court rejected the claim of discriminatory pricing.

90. Turning to the private enforcement claims digital sector in relation to the Google Shopping case.[31] As a reminder of facts of the public enforcement case, on the 30th of November 2010 the EU Commission initiated a formal investigation proceeding against Google after receiving number of complaints. On the 27th of June 2017, the EU Commission fined 2.42 billion euros Google for infringement to Article 101 TFEU. Google abused its dominance in the relevant markets for general search services by positioning and displaying more favourably its own comparison-shopping service compared to competition comparison shopping services in its general search results pages. On the 10th of November 2021 the General Court released a judgment

30 For a cross analysis of mobile virtual network operators competitive strategies and performance in Italy and France see Corrocher and Lasio (2013). Some of these operators were sued for damages and their cases are referred in the database of this essay.

31 AT.39740.

dismissing Google's action for annulment and upheld the fine. On the 20 January 2022, Google and Alphabet launched an appeal against the judgment of the General Court, putting forward four grounds of appeals. On the 11th of January 2024 the Advocate General Kokott delivered her opinion, proposing that the Court of Justice dismisses the appeal. In the dataset of this essay, three private enforcement cases were launched in the UK, from Infederation, Whitewater and Kelkoo.[32] Infederation ("Foundem") lodged a complaint against Google with the Commission on the 3rd of November 2009, which was then replaced by a new version and the non-confidential version was submitted to Google on the 10th of February 2010. On the 7th of December, Foundem also applied for leave to intervene in support of the form of order sought by the Commission. Foundem first issued a private enforcement claim in 2012, but then made several successive amendments. On the 22nd of February 2019 a revised claim was served with additional references to the recitals in the 2017 Commission Decision. The High Court of Justice, in its decision of 18 March 2020, qualifies Foundem's claim as an "hybrid claim", since it is partially a follow-on claim relying on the infringement of Article 102 in the Commission decision and partially a stand-alone claim alleging further grounds of infringements. The claim was transferred to the Competition Appeal Tribunal on the 16th of May 2023. Interestingly, from the 26th of May ruling from the CAT, on a request from Foundem to have Google disclosing data, one can learned that the four on-going damages claims against Google are now being managed together, including a claim that does not figure in this essay's dataset, from Connexity, which was transferred to the CAT on the 11th of March 2024. Furthermore, still from the 16th of May 2023 ruling, the CAT notes that Foundem's pleading, only sets out a claim for loss in general terms with a one-page schedule of figures but it is not clear from either of those documents how Foundem will approach quantification. Therefore, the CAT "expect Foundem, over the coming months, to instruct its economist to address in more detail the way in which Foundem intends to approach quantification and the method that he intends to use." (§13). Kelkoo, same as Infederation, took part in the public enforcement proceedings of the Google Shopping case. In the decision from the Commission, Kelkoo submitted his application to be heard as a third party and 2017, two months after Google brought the action for annulment, Kelkoo applied for leave to intervene in support of the form of order sought by the Commission. In November 2021, the private enforcement proceedings were transferred from the High

32 While this section focuses on private enforcement related to the Google Shopping case, in the UK, Ms Nikki Stopford initiated in October 2023 proceedings for a class action in relation to the Google Android case. In Italy, Attrakt succeeded in bringing a damages' claim against Google in relation to the Google Adsense case.

Court to the CAT. In March 2023 a ruling was hold on the disclosure of documents in relation to pre-decision EU Commission file. Lastly, Whitewater, which is a subsidiary of Kelkoo, and which acquired the comparison shopping service "Ciao" requested damages for loss of revenues from Google's abusive practices impacting the traffic volume. Interestingly, the summary of the claim notes that the 2017 Google Shopping decision from the Commission is not a final infringement decision but still the Tribunal must have regard to the decision as being a relevant decision of the Commission made before IP Completion Day (i.e. Brexit). According to the summary of the claim, if the Court of Justice dismisses the defendants' appeal, then it will become a final infringement decision.

91. The "finality" of the Google decision was also in the core of the dispute following the private enforcement claim introduced by 7 Pixel in Italy. On the 4th of January 2021, the Court of Milan rejected a request from 7 Pixel, operating in the Italian market for e-merchant product comparison services, for a preventive technical expertise. The preventive technical expertise is a tool from the Italian Code of Civil procedure, which allows to establish the existence and amount of monetary damages, with the aim to resolve the dispute through conciliation (Pietrini, 2021). Google opposed the request, stressing that the Commission decision was not final. The Court rejected the use of the tool it cannot be used when the decision requires verification of facts and analysis of complex legal issues beyond a technical investigation. In this case, the question of the proof and duration of infringement, and causal link were raised, therefore the action for damages must be analysed on the merits. Finally, in France, on the 7th of January 2020, the *Cour d'appel de Paris*, ruled out a claim for lack of jurisdiction raised by Google, in the private enforcement action brought by LeGuide. Google claimed that the competence of the *Court d'appel de Paris* was neither justified as the basis of the domicile of one of the co-defendants nor as the place where the damage occurred, additionally noting that LeGuide requested the compensation for a damage for which a part occurred in France and another part in other Member States. Google further argued that damages were suffered where it occurred, and in that case, since it consists of a drop-in traffic and redirection of customers to its websites aimed at a foreign audience, generating a loss of income to its website, the damage did not manifest in France but in these other countries (§23). Finally, Google added that, in the matter of damage suffered on the internet, the territorial jurisdiction is determined according to the territory for which the websites are and for which the websites are intended (§24). LeGuide opposed that since the dispute concerns the infringement to Article 102 TFEU, EU competition rules would be undermined if infringers were able to artificially fragment litigation (§31).

92. The *Cour d'Appel de Paris*, applying Article 7 (2) of Regulation Bruxelles 1, ruled that the market affected by the abusive conduct must that the market where LeGuide develops, operates price comparison services and records traffic on its sites and not the one for which the sites are intended (§54). Furthermore, the location of LeGuide registered office, which can also be considered a relevant criterion, corresponds to the place where the damage materialised, even if its activity is directed towards internet users in several European countries, which makes it possible to avoid fragmentation of the same dispute between several jurisdictions (§57). Interestingly, the *Cour d'Appel de Paris* confirmed the decision Tribunal de commerce, which granted Google a request for a stay of proceedings until a final decision by the EU Courts in the Google Shopping case and dismissing LeGuide requests for production of documents. From the cross-analysis of these damages claims following the Google Shopping cases, several observations can be drawn. First, considering the duration of the public enforcement cases, only "exploited" companies, still on the market, might have the resources to bring claims, considering that there is not yet a final decision, which is a clear strategy from Google to delay claims for damages. Second, claimants must be armed against the creativity from Google's lawyers in raising lack of jurisdiction claims to achieve fragmentation but also must be armed to face the challenge of quantifying the quantum of damages in a complex infringement, especially should their access to documents be dismissed.

93. Finally, in terms of limits of this analysis, this essay tries to measure the determinants of a litigated case. However, litigated cases are not representative of all the legal disputes or abuse of dominant behaviours. As such, the analysis is subject to an inherent selection bias, as claimants are more likely to bring a case when they expect a favourable outcome and can bear the costs of litigation. Consequently, unsuccessful or marginal claims are likely to be underrepresented in the dataset. In the database, the cases are not unevenly distributed between years, economic sectors, and countries, which may affect the generalisability of the results. Finally, given potential endogeneity concerns, future research would benefit from the collection of more granular data, which could allow for more refined empirical strategies.

1.6 Conclusion

94. The purpose of this essay is to fill in the gap in the empirical literature on damages actions for abuse of dominance position with the policy perspective of the upcoming damages actions in digital markets. Therefore, this essay relies on an original database of 194 cases of damages actions following a claimed infringement to Article 102 in France,

United Kingdom, and Italy. In terms of method, a logistical regression estimates the probability of successful damages' cases, and five hypotheses were drawn to test the determinants of success.

95. Contrary to previous studies mapping damages actions following infringements of Article 101 TFEU, the results indicate that follow-on actions relating to abuse of dominance under Article 102 TFEU are associated with a lower likelihood of success than stand-alone actions. This finding points to differences in the litigation of damages actions between infringements of Articles 101 and 102 TFEU. No clear association is identified between the type of relief sought and the outcome of damages actions. This may reflect the fact that, for claimants, seeking injunctive relief and claiming monetary damages are not mutually exclusive strategies. The introduction of the Damages Directive and its transposition are positively and statistically associated with successful outcomes in damages actions. With respect to economic sectors, claims brought in the information and communication sector and in the transport sector are associated with a lower likelihood of success compared to claims in other sectors included in the database. When considering whether sectoral case concentration, used as a proxy for a potential learning effect, is related to case outcomes, the estimated association differs across jurisdictions: the likelihood of success is higher for damages cases in France but lower for damages cases in Italy. Finally, with regard to the digital sector, claims introduced in this sector are associated with a lower likelihood of success, this result is more pronounced in Italy. However, when interacting the digital sector variable with the log-linearised amount of damages, the interaction term is positive and statistically significant, suggesting that the relationship between digital-sector claims and case outcomes may depend on the scale of the damages sought.

96. This analysis, of the determinants of successful damages claims for an abuse of dominance is particularly relevant in the light of the past, on-going, and up-coming enforcement strategy of abuse of dominance in digital markets. Indeed, these cases, as it was exemplified with the Google Shopping cases, are likely to have caused widespread damages, to hundreds if not thousands of business users, in several countries. Furthermore, still taking the example of Alphabet, considering the several competition law public enforcement cases, both at the EU and national level, and an-going DMA compliance for which an investigation was opened for potential non-compliance with Article 6(5) of the DMA prohibiting self-preferencing,[33] there is a clear need need for complementary private enforcement mechanisms to contribute to deterring abuses of dominance in digital markets. Therefore, putting in perspective the results of this essay, damages actions in the digital

33 Press release from the EU Commission: https://ec.europa.eu/commission/presscorner/detail/en/ip_24_1689

sector will benefit from the harmonisation of the rules brought by the Damages Directive. While follow-on actions are less successful, this essay makes the hypothesis that it could be linked to lengthier and fewer public enforcement cases following infringements to Article 102 than 102 TFEU. Therefore, considering again the Google Shopping case that is still on-going and for which the EU Commission initiated proceedings on 30 November 2010, it will be most interesting to monitor the outcomes of the on-going private enforcement cases in digital markets. Furthermore, aiming to achieve faster compliance with an *ex-ante* regulation, the private enforcement of the DMA could be an alternative for business users whose harm is resulting from infringements of the obligations of the DMA. In particular, the DMA could make up for the lack of harmonised collective actions in the Damages Directive (Hornkohl and Ribera Martínez, 2023). Many of the proposals in the literature to improve private enforcement of competition law in general are held for the digital markets, for examples: injunctions (Cauffman, 2010), expert judges (Hornkohl, 2022), collective actions (Gaudin and Weber, 2021). However, private enforcement of competition law also raises specific challenges in digital markets, among which, the quantification of the harm if the action is raised by consumers on zero-priced market or the lack of presumption of harm in the Damages Directive for abuse of dominance for both businesses and consumers bringing damages claims. The question also remains open as to whether the new set of guidelines on Article 102 TFEU could be beneficial for stand-alone cases following an abuse of dominance.

97. It would be relevant to pursue this research analysis with both a larger sample of cases, collecting data on more than three countries, but also collecting data at a more granular level, for example, including the market share of the companies, the judges, structure of the lawyer fee, and information on the quantification of damages. In terms of method, this essay collects data on private enforcement cases. While relying on observed data for practical reasons, another aspect of litigation is not measured: the number of unobserved private settlement, dropped cases or non-reported cases. In addition, as Peyer (2012), puts it, a few numbers of damages cases could either indicate a strong public enforcement (with little abuse of dominance breaches to compensate for) or a very weak private enforcement with no incentives to introduce actions. Therefore, as he suggested in his study, another approach could have been to assess how many private enforcement cases for an anticompetitive conduct sanctioned under public enforcement, which would allow to obtain a ratio of follow-on and stand-alone cases, as an indicator of non-effectiveness in terms of incentives. Going further, this approach could also be applied as the next step of this research.

1.7 Bibliography

Allain, Marie-Laure, Boyer, Marcel and Ponssard, Jean Pierre. "The Determination of Optimal Fines in Cartel Cases: Theory and Practice." *Concurrences* 4 (2011): 32-40.

Baker, Jonathan B. "Private information and the deterrent effect of antitrust damage remedies." *The Journal of Law, Economics, and Organization* 4, no. 2 (1988): 385-408.

Becker, Gary S. "Crime and punishment: an economic approach." *Journal of Political Economy* 76, no. 2 (1968): 169-217.

Bernardeau, Ludovic. "Action privée : La Cour de justice de l'Union européenne apporte des précisions sur l'application dans le temps de la directive 2014/104/UE et sur la conformité au droit de l'Union européenne de dispositions de droit interne relatives à la prescription des actions en dommages et intérêts, antérieures à la transposition de ladite directive (*Cogeco / Sport TV Portugal*). " no.2 Concurrences (2019):152.

Besanko, David and Daniel F. Spulber. "Are treble damages neutral? sequential equilibrium and private antitrust enforcement." *The American Economic Review* (1990): 870-887.

Bien, F., F. Wagner-von Papp, A. S. Choné-Grimaldi, S. Pietrini, R. Amaro, A. Bass, P. Camesasca, P. Hitchings, L. Loras, and M. Angel Malo. "La transposition de la directive 2014/104/UE relative aux actions en dommages et intérêts pour violation du droit des pratiques anticoncurrentielles. " *Concurrences*, (2015): 11-37.

Boulu-Reshef, Béatrice and Constance Monnier-Schlumberger. "Lutte contre les cartels: comment dissuader les têtes brûlées? " *Revue Économique* 70, no. 6 (2019): 1187-1199.

Carval, Suzanne and Laborde, Jean-François. "La réparation des préjudices causés par les abus de position dominante. " *Concurrences* (2018) N° 1-2018, Art. N° 84883.

Cauffman, Caroline. "Injunctions at the request of third parties in EU competition law." *Maastricht Journal of European and Comparative Law* 17.1 (2010): 58-86.

Combe, Emmanuel and Constance Monnier. "Fines against hard core cartels in europe: the myth of overenforcement." *The Antitrust Bulletin* 56, no. 2 (2011): 235-275.

Cooter, Robert D. and Daniel L. Rubinfeld. "Economic analysis of legal disputes and their resolution." *Journal of Economic Literature* 27, no. 3 (1989): 1067-1097.

Corrocher, Nicoletta, and Laura Lasio. "Diversification strategies in network-based services: The case of mobile virtual network operators." Telecommunications Policy 37, no. 11 (2013): 1110-1123.

Dau-Schmidt, Kenneth G.; Gallo, Joseph; Parker, Charles; and Craycraft, Joseph, "Criminal penalties under the Sherman act: a study of law and economics." *Articles by Maurer Faculty* (1994). 654.

Davis, Joshua P. and Robert H. Lande. "Benefits from private antitrust enforcement: forty individual case studies." *University of San Francisco Law Research Paper* no. 2011-22 (2008).

Davis, Joshua P. and Robert H. Lande. "Toward an empirical and theoretical assessment of private antitrust enforcement." *Seattle UL Rev.* 36, (2013): 1269.

European Commission, Directorate-General for Competition. "Study on the conditions of claims for damages in case of infringement of EC competition rules: comparative and economics reports." (2004).

European Commission. "Directive 2014/104/EU of the European Parliament and of the Council of 26 November 2014 on certain rules governing actions for damages under national law for infringements of the competition law provisions of the Member States and of the European Union Text with EEA relevance." (2014) *OJ L 349, 5.12.2014, p. 1–19.*

European Commission. "Staff working document on the implementation of Directive 2014/104/EU of the European Parliament and of the Council of 26 November 2014 on certain rules governing actions for damages under national law for infringements of the competition law provisions of the Member States and of the European Union". SWD (2020) 338 final.

Gaudin, Germain, and Franziska Weber. "Antitrust damages, consumer harm, and consumer collective redress." *Journal of European Competition Law & Practice* 12.5 (2021): 370-379.

Hornkohl, Lena. "Leave it to the experts: A comparative analysis of competition-expert lay judges in private enforcement of competition law." *Yearbook of Antitrust and Regulatory Studies (YARS)* 15.25 (2022): 7-36.

Hornkohl, Lena, and Alba Ribera Martínez. "Collective Actions and the Digital Markets Act: A Bird Without Wings." *Available at SSRN 4637661* (2023).

Hüschelrath, Kai. "Public and private enforcement of competition law: a differentiated approach." *World Competition* 36, no. 4 (2013).

Janin, Lionel and Benoît Menoni. "Le contrôle des concentrations en France: une analyse empirique des avis du conseil de la concurrence." *Economie et Prévision* 178179, no. 2 (2007): 93-114.

Kahneman, Daniel. "A perspective on judgment and choice: mapping bounded rationality." *American Psychologist* 58, no. 9 (2003): 697.

Laborde, Jean-François. "Cartel damages actions in Europe: how courts have assessed cartel overcharges (2021 Ed.)." *Concurrences* 03-2021, (2021): 232-242.

Lande, Robert H. "Are antitrust treble damages really single damages." *Ohio State Law Journal.* 26 (1996): 463.

Landes, William M. "Optimal sanctions for antitrust violations." *The University of Chicago Law Review* 50, no. 2 (1983): 652-678.

Lauk, Martina. "Ökonometrische analyse der entscheidungspraxis Des Bundeskartellamtes." *Darmstadt Discussion Papers in Economics,* (2003). https://www.econstor.eu/handle/10419/84839/.

Francisco, Marcos. "The Spanish Supreme Court sentences the truck cartel." *Kluwer Competition Law Blog*, (2023).

Marvel, Howard P., Jeffry M. Netter, and Anthony M. Robinson. "Price fixing and civil damages: An economic analysis." *Stanford Law Review* (1988): 561-575.

McAfee, R. Preston, Hugo M. Mialon, and Sue H. Mialon. "Private v. public antitrust enforcement: a strategic analysis." *Journal of Public Economics* 92, no. 10-11 (2008): 1863-1875.

O'Donoghue, Robert. "Europe's long march towards antitrust damages actions." *CPI Antitrust Chronicle* no. 2 (2011).

Pénard, Thierry and Souam, Saïd. "Que peut bien apporter l'analyse économique à l'application du droit de la concurrence ?" *Revue d'Economie Politique* 112, no. 6 (2002): 863-887.

Perloff, Jeffrey M., Daniel L. Rubinfeld, and Paul Ruud. "Antitrust settlements and trial outcomes." *The Review of Economics and Statistics* (1996): 401-409.

Peyer, Sebastian. "Private antitrust litigation in Germany from 2005 to 2007: empirical evidence." *Journal of Competition Law and Economics* 8, no. 2 (2012): 331-359.

Pietrini, Silvia. "Le Tribunal de Milan rejette une demande d'expertise technique visant à mettre un terme au contentieux concurrentiel par le biais d'une conciliation (*7 Pixel / Google*). " *Concurrences* N° 3-2021, Art. N° 101658, (2021) pp. 214-215.

Polinsky, A. Mitchell and Shavell, Steven. "The optimal use of fines and imprisonment." *Journal of Public Economics* 24, no. 1 (1984): 89-99.

Rodger, Barry J. "Competition law litigation in the UK Courts: a study of all cases 2005-2008-Part I." *Global Competition Litigation Review* (2009): 93-114.

Rodger, Barry J. "Private enforcement of competition law, the hidden story Part II: Competition litigation settlements in the UK, 2008-2012." *Global Competition Litigation Review* 8, no. 3 (2015): 89-108.

Salant, Stephen W. "Treble damage awards in private lawsuits for price fixing." *Journal of Political Economy* 95, no. 6 (1987): 1326-1336.

Segal, Ilya R. and Michael D. Whinston. "Public vs. private enforcement of antitrust law: a survey." *Stanford Law and Economics Olin Working Paper* No. 335 (2006).

Sousa Ferro, Miguel. "Jurisprudência de 'private enforcement' (Private Enforcement Case-Law)." *Jurisprudência Portuguesa De Direito Da Concorrência Capítulo* 7, (2016).

Tversky, Amos and Daniel Kahneman. "Rational choice and the framing of decisions." In *Multiple Criteria Decision Making and Risk Analysis using Microcomputers*, 81-126: Springer, 1989.

Wils, Wouter PJ. "Private enforcement of eu antitrust law and its relationship with public enforcement: past, present and future." *World Competition* (2017): 27.

Wils, Wouter PJ. "Should private antitrust enforcement be encouraged in Europe?" *World Competition* 26, no. 3 (2003).

1.8 List of figures

1.9 List of tables

1.10 Annex: List of cases

COUNTRY	COURT	PARTIES	REFERENCE	DATE OF THE LAST DECISION IN THE DATABASE
FRANCE	Cour de Cassation	SNVC et al. c/ Société France Régions 3 "F.R.3"	No. 94-17.410	21/05/1996
FRANCE	Cour de Cassation	SARL Les Sablières de Guadeloupe et al. c/ SA Somatco	RG 9400036	21/10/1997
ITALY	Corte di Cassazione	Soc. Unimare c. Soc. GE.A.SAR e altro	No. 6368	17/05/2000
UNITED KINGDOM	High Court of Justice	Synstar Computer Services (United Kingdom) Ltd v ICL	[2001] EWHC 569 (Ch)	30/03/2001
UNITED KINGDOM	High Court of Justice	Getmapping Plc v Ordnance Survey	[2002] EWHC 1089 (Pat)	31/05/2002
FRANCE	Cour d'Appel de Paris	SARL P. Streiff Motorsport et al. c/ SAS Speedy	RG 2000-10676	28/06/2002
UNITED KINGDOM	Supreme Court of Judicature, Court of Appeal	Intel Corporation v Via Technologies Inc & Ors	[2002] EWCA Civ 1905	20/12/2002
ITALY	Corte d'Appello di Roma	Soc. Albacom c. Soc. Telecom Italia		20/01/2003
FRANCE	Cour d'Appel de Versailles	Verimedia v. SA Médiamétrie, SA Sedicop, GIE Audipub et al.	No. 2002-07434	24/06/2004
UNITED KINGDOM	High Court of Justice	Arkin v Borchard Lines Ltd & Ors	[2005] EWCA Civ 655	26/05/2005
ITALY	Corte d'Appello di Milano	Exergia S.p.A. c. Trans Tunisian Pipeline Company Limited		10/01/2006
ITALY	Corte d'Appello di Milano	CO.TRA.GE.MO c. Logista Italia	No. 384	13/04/2006
FRANCE	Cour d'Appel de Paris	Société LUnited Kingdom Lamellen Und Kupplungsbau Gmbh / SA Valeo	No. 05/10916	10/05/2006

ITALY	Corte d'Appello di Milano	Telextra S.r.l. c. Telecom Italia S.p.A.	No. 788	25/05/2006
UNITED KINGDOM	High Court of Justice	Ineos Vinyls Ltd.& Ors v Huntsman Petrochemicals	[2006] EWHC 1241	26/05/2006
UNITED KINGDOM	High Court of Justice	Adidas-Salomon Ag v Drape & Ors	[2006] EWHC 1318	07/06/2006
UNITED KINGDOM	High Court of Justice	P & S Amusements Ltd v Valley House Leisure Ltd & Anor	[2006] EWHC 1510	26/06/2006
UNITED KINGDOM	Competition Appeal Tribunal	Healthcare at Home v Genzyme Ltd	[2006] CAT 29	15/11/2006
UNITED KINGDOM	Court of Appeal	Attheraces Ltd & Anor v The British Horseracing Board Ltd & Anor Rev 2 [2007] EWCA Civ 38	[2007] EWCA Civ 38	02/02/2007
UNITED KINGDOM	High Court of Justice	Sandisk Corporation v Koninklijke Philips Electronics NV & Ors	Sandisk Corporation v Koninklijke Philips Electronics NV & Ors [2007] EWHC 332 (Ch)	27/02/2007
UNITED KINGDOM	High Court of Justice	AAH Pharmaceuticals Ltd & Ors v Pfizer Ltd & Anor	[2007] EWHC 565 (Ch)	05/03/2007
UNITED KINGDOM	High Court of Justice	English Welsh & Scottish Railway Ltd v E. On United Kingdom Plc & Anor	[2007] EWHC 599 (Comm)	23/03/2007
UNITED KINGDOM	High Court of Justice	Chester City Council & Anor v Arriva Plc & Ors	[2007] EWHC 1373	15/06/2007
ITALY	Corte d'Appello di Milano	Fly c. Sea	No. 287	04/07/2007
UNITED KINGDOM	High Court of Justice	Software Cellular Network Ltd v T-Mobile (United Kingdom) Ltd	[2007] EWHC 1790 (Ch)	17/07/2007
UNITED KINGDOM	High Court of Justice	Hutchinson 3G United Kingdom Ltd v O2 (United Kingdom) Ltd & Ors	[2008] EWHC 50 (Comm)	18/01/2008

ITALY	Corte d'Appello di Milano	Petrone Farmacie c. Pharmacia Italia e Pfizer	No. 8353	20/02/2008
UNITED KINGDOM	Supreme Court of Judicature, Court of Appeal	British Sky Broadcasting Group Plc & Anor v Virgin Media Communications Ltd & Ors	[2008] EWCA Civ 612	06/06/2008
FRANCE	Cour d'Appel de Montpellier	Unilia Mutuelle Santé Prévoyance c/ Groupe Languedoc – Mutualité Mutuelle	No 09-01917	09/03/2010
UNITED KINGDOM	High Court of Justice	Humber Oil v. Associated British Ports	[2011] EWHC 352 (Ch)	24/02/2011
FRANCE	Tribunal de Commerce	SAS Numéricable, SA NC Numéricable, SAS Est Vidéocommunication v. SA France Telecom – Orange (n°2009-073089)	No. 2009-073089	30/03/2011
UNITED KINGDOM	High Court of Justice	Purple Parking Ltd & Anor v Heathrow Airport Ltd	[2011] EWHC 987 (Ch)	15/04/2011
FRANCE	Cour d'Appel de Paris	Mr. M. c/ SNC Société Presse Paris Services SPPS	RG 08-21750	27/04/2011
UNITED KINGDOM	Competition Appeal Tribunal	Enron Coal Services Limited (in liquidation) v English Welsh & Scottish Railway Limited	1106/5/7/08	28/06/2011
FRANCE	Tribunal de commerce de Paris	SA Dufry France c/ SNC Relay France RG	2005049045	27/09/2011
UNITED KINGDOM	High Court of Justice	Transport for London v. John Griffin, Addison Lee PLC, Eventech Limited	HQ12X01527	26/04/2012
UNITED KINGDOM	United Kingdom Competition Appeal Tribunal	2 Travel Group PLC (in liquidation) v Cardiff City Transport Services Limited	1178/5/711	05/07/2012

ITALY	Corte d'Appello di Roma	Fallimento Intratec Spa In Liquidazione	No. 1356	11/03/2013
UNITED KINGDOM	United Kingdom Competition Appeal Tribunal	Albion Water v Dwr Cymru	1166/5/7/10	28/03/2013
ITALY	Tribunale di Milano	Viaggiare s.r.l. / Ryanair Ltd.	No. 7825	04/06/2013
UNITED KINGDOM	High Court of Justice	Dahabshiil Transfer Services / Barclays Bank	HC13E04616	05/11/2013
UNITED KINGDOM	Court of Appeal	Chemistree Homecare Limited v. Abbvie Limited	[2013] EWCA Civ 1338	07/11/2013
UNITED KINGDOM	High Court of Justice	Arriva The Shires Ltd v. London Luton Airport Operations Ltd	HC13D01784	28/01/2014
UNITED KINGDOM	High Court of Justice	Reckitt Benckiser		01/02/2014
ITALY	Tribunale di Milano	Intermatica S.p.A. / Telecom Italia S.p.A.	No. 6621	14/05/2014
ITALY	Corte di Cassazione	Consorzio Tutela del Grana Padano c. Valgrana	No. 1801	16/05/2014
ITALY	Corte d'Appello di Milano	S.M. / M-Dis Distribuzione Media / Mdm Milano Distribuzione Media	No. 2050	04/06/2014
FRANCE	Cour d'Appel de Paris	SA La Montagne c/ SAS Aviscom	RG 12-10322	17/09/2014
FRANCE	Cour d'Appel de Paris	Me S. (mandataire liquidateur) et al. c/ la Monnaie de Paris	RG 13-00265	30/10/2014
ITALY	Tribunale di Milano	Delta Air Lines / Iberia Linee Aeree Spagnole / TAP – Air Portugal / Società per azioni Esercizi Aeroportuali S.E.A.	No. 15054	17/12/2014
ITALY	Corte d'Appello di Roma	Tecnomatch / Matches & Flames	No. 1072	17/02/2015
ITALY	Supreme Court of Cassation	Comi S.r.l. et al. / Cargest S.r.l.	No. 11564	04/06/2015

UNITED KINGDOM	High Court of Justice	Packet Media Ltd v Telefonica	[2015] EWHC 2235 (Ch)	20/07/2015
ITALY	Corte d'Appello di Milano	RIBES / AGENZIA delle Entrate	No. 3374	04/08/2015
FRANCE	Cour d'Appel de Paris	Rocca Transports SARL v. Société Nationale Maritime Corse Méditerranée (SNCM)	RG 14/03665	22/10/2015
FRANCE	Cour d'Appel de Paris	Société Evermaps v. SARL Google France, Société Google Inc.	No. 12/02931	25/11/2015
FRANCE	Corte d'Appel de Paris	Société Aviscom c/ SA Ouest France et al.	RG 14-05555	26/11/2015
ITALY	Tribunale di Milano	M. C. S. / FIERA MILANO	No. 13484	01/12/2015
ITALY	Tribunale di Milano	Arslogica Sistemi S.r.l./ IBM Italia S.p.A.	No. 4620	24/12/2015
ITALY	Corte d'Appello di Milano	OKCom S.p.A / Telecom Italia S.p.A	No. 4986	28/12/2015
ITALY	Tribunale di Milano	Volare / Kai / S.E.A.	No. 14783	28/12/2015
ITALY	Corte d'Appello di Milano	Studio Gatti / Agenzia Delle Entrate e del Territorio	No. 9	07/01/2016
ITALY	Corte d'Appello di Milano	Brennercom / Telecom Italia	No. 334	01/02/2016
UNITED KINGDOM	High Court of Justice	Streetmap.eu Limited v Google Inc, Google Ireland Limited and Google United Kingdom Limited	HC-2013-000090	12/02/2016
FRANCE	Cour d'Appel de Paris	Le Berry Républicain et al. c/ SAS Aviscom	RG 14-11095	22/03/2016
ITALY	Tribunale di Milano	Eutelia S.p.A. / Vodafone Omnitel N.V. S.p.A., No. 4255	No. 4255	05/04/2016

FRANCE	Cour d'Appel de Paris	SARL Imperial Pub, SARL GPS v. SA La Poste, SAS MediaPost (n°13/24840)	No. 13/24840	13/04/2016
ITALY	Corte d'Appello di Roma	G. E. A. S. R. L., / A.I.A. – Associazione Italiana Allevatori / As.Na.Co.Di – Associazione Nazionale Condifesa / Willis Italia	No. 2408	16/04/2016
ITALY	Corte d'Appello di Milano	Vodafone Omnitel / Teleunit	No. 2108	27/05/2016
ITALY	Corte d'Appello di Milano	Uno Communications / Telecom Italia	No. 2179	31/05/2016
FRANCE	Tribunal de Commerce de Paris	GIE Pari Mutuel Urbain c/ SARL Google France, Société Google Inc. et al.	RG 2016035909	20/06/2016
ITALY	Corte d'Appello di Roma	Unasca – Unione Nazionale Autoscuole E Studi Di Consulenza Automobilistica / Aci – Automobile Club D'italia	No. 4314	07/07/2016
ITALY	Tribunale di Milano	Attrakt / Google Ireland	No. 7638	17/07/2016
ITALY	Corte d'Appello di Milano	Uno Communications / Vodafone Omnitel	No. 3052	21/07/2016
ITALY	Tribunale civile di Roma	FALLIMENTO Della Spa F.E.R.V.E.T. Fabbrica E Riparazioni Vagoni E Tramways / TRENITALIA	No. 17714	26/09/2016
ITALY	Tribunale di Milano	Industrias Afrasa / Bayer Cropscience	No. 11169	12/10/2016

FRANCE	Cour d'Appel de Paris	Aviscom v. SA La Montagne, SAS Centre France Publicité, SAS Dans nos coeurs	RG 14/01036	07/12/2016
FRANCE	Cour d'Appel de Paris	SAS Pétanque Longue c/ SAS La Boule Obut	RG 16/15228	07/12/2016
ITALY	Corte d'Appello di Milano	Brennercom S.p.A / Telecom Italia S.p.A., No. 16319, General Registry 22423/2010	No. 1/2017	02/01/2017
FRANCE	Cour d'Appel Fort-de-France	C. c/ SARL Cinésogar SARL Filmdis, SAS Mediagestion	RG 15/00486	24/01/2017
ITALY	Corte d'Appello di Roma	Net – Tyre / Michelin Italiana	No. 747	06/02/2017
ITALY	Corte d'Appello di Roma	Alba 90 S.R.L. In Liquidazione / Enel S.P.A., Enel Distribuzione S.P.A. Ed Enel Factor S.P.A.	No. 1043	16/02/2017
ITALY	Corte d'Appello di Milano	Fastweb Spa / Vodafone Omnitel N.V. Spa	No. 887	01/03/2017
ITALY	Corte d'Appello di Milano	Strano? Stranissimo! Di A. S. & C. / A.D.G. Ser	No. 1573	09/03/2017
FRANCE	Cour de Cassation chambre commerciale	Cowes	No. 15-28.197	26/04/2017
FRANCE	Cour d'Appel de Paris	SAS Outremer Telecom v. SA Orange Caraïbe (	No. 15/05918	10/05/2017
UNITED KINGDOM	United Kingdom Competition Appeal Tribunal	Socrates Training Limited v The Law Society of England and Wales	1249/5/7/16	26/05/2017
ITALY	Corte d'Appello di Milano	Societa' Esercizi Aeroportuali Spa / Saudi Arabian Airlines	No. 2561	09/06/2017

ITALY	Corte d'Appello di Milano	Societa' Esercizi Aeroportuali Spa / Nippon Cargo Airlines	No. 2658	15/06/2017
ITALY	Corte d'Appello di Milano	Swiss International Airline S.p.A. / SEA Società esercizi aeroportuali S.p.A.,No. 7970	No. 3378	18/07/2017
ITALY	Tribunale di Roma	Ministry of Health and Ministry of Economy and Finance / Pfizer Italia S.r.l.	No. 15020	24/07/2017
ITALY	Corte d'Appello di Milano	Airline Logistic S.r.l., Globe Air Cargo S.r.l., Swissport Cargo Services Italia S.r.l., Worldair S.r.l., Sasco S.r.l. / SEA S.p.A., No. 3324	No. 3539	29/07/2017
FRANCE	Cour d'Appel de Paris	SAS Central Parts v. JCB Sales	No. 12/04441	20/09/2017
ITALY	Tribunale di Milano	Next Mind / Vodafone Italia	No. 12344	06/12/2017
FRANCE	Cour d'Appel de Paris	SARL DKT International v. SA ECO-Emballages, SA Valorplast	No. 15/07266	20/12/2017
ITALY	Corte d'Appello di Milano	Societa' Esercizi Aeroportuali Spa / Continental Airlines, Oggi Denominata United Airlines Inc	No. 5421/2017	27/12/2017
ITALY	Corte d'Appello di Milano	Societa' Esercizi Aeroportuali Spa / Saudi Arabian Airlines / Continental Airlines	No. 50	09/01/2018
ITALY	Corte d'Appello di Milano	Societa' Per Azioni Esercizi Aeroportuali / Cismat	No. 688	08/02/2018
ITALY	Tribunale di Milano	Max Bet Sas Di Conte Paolo & C. / Cirsa Italia	No. 2108	26/02/2018

ITALY	Tribunale di Milano	Teleunit S.p.A. / Telecom Italia S.p.A.	No. 8008, General Registry 76561/2008	08/03/2018
ITALY	Corte d'Appello di Milano	Societa' Per Azioni Esercizi Aeroportuali / Air Kosmo / Latasped / La Minerva / Cad Mollica	No. 1370	20/03/2018
ITALY	Corte d'Appello di Milano	BT Italia S.p.A. / Vodafone Omnitel N.V.	No. 9109	26/03/2018
FRANCE	Cour d'Appel de Paris	Lectiel v. SA Orange	No.14/14758	11/04/2018
ITALY	Tribunale di Milano	Dari Medical / F. Hoffmann-La Roche	No. 4592	23/04/2018
ITALY	Corte d'Appello di Milano	Sea Societa' Esercizi Aeroportuali / Antonelli Transit Air Malpensa / Laser / Ceva Freight Italy / Aviosped	No. 2490	18/05/2018
ITALY	Tribunale di Roma	Saraceni Automobili / Toyota Motor Italia	No. 11737	07/06/2018
FRANCE	Tribunal de Commerce de Paris	SA Orange Réunion c/ SRR and SFR	RG 2014058853	25/06/2018
ITALY	Corte d'Appello di Milano	S.E.A. Società Esercizi Aeroportuali / Battaglino / Shenker italiana / First international	No. 3450	17/07/2018
ITALY	Corte d'Appello di Milano	Brussels Airlines, American Alrlines, Royal Jordanian, Aegean Alrljnes / Sea Società Esel~Cizi Aeroportuali	No.3643	27/07/2018
ITALY	Tribunale di Roma	L. N. D. / Italiana Petroli	No. 16195	03/08/2018
FRANCE	Cour d'Appel de Paris	Betclic v. PMU	No. 18/04914	12/09/2018

ITALY	Corte d'Appello di Milano	Sea Società Esercizi Aeroportuali / Airlines Representative Europe	No. 4115/2018	14/09/2018
ITALY	Corte d'Appello di Roma	Fastweb / Wind Tre	No. 5936	25/09/2018
UNITED KINGDOM	High Court of Justice	Apple Retail United Kingdom Limited and others v Qualcomm United Kingdom Limited and Qualcomm Incorporated	HP-2017-000015	01/10/2018
UNITED KINGDOM	High Court of Justice	Apple v. Qualcomm	[2018] EWHC 2711 (Ch)	16/10/2018
ITALY	Tribunale ordinario di Roma	A-Tono / Telecom Italia	No. 22166	16/11/2018
FRANCE	Cour d'Appel de Paris	Sté Inforad Limited c/ SASU Coyote System	RG 17/00219	19/12/2018
ITALY	Tribunale di Roma	Esperia / Enel Distribuzion	No. 787	11/01/2019
FRANCE	Cour de Cassation 1ère chambre civile	Apple eBizcuss	No. 14-16.898	30/01/2019
FRANCE	Cour d'Appel de Paris	SASU Fibre Excellence Tarascon and SAS Bioenerg c/ SA ERDF (now Enedis)	RG 16/06164	08/02/2019
FRANCE	Cour d'Appel de Paris	Sarl Arkeos, Sarl Cap Eco Energie, Sarl Apem Energie, Sarl Sol'air Confort, Sas Gavriane, Sarl Cap Sud France v. EDF (SA Electricité de France, SASU EDF Energies Nouvelles Réparties, SASU EDF ENR Solaire)	No. 17/21261	06/03/2019
ITALY	Tribunale civile di Roma	Kpnqwest Italia / Telecom Italia	No. 9115	30/04/2019

UNITED KINGDOM	High Court United Kingdom Competition Appeal Tribunal	Unlockd Ltd and Unlockd Media Technology Ltd v Google Ireland Ltd, Google Commerce Ltd and Google LLC	1283/5/7/18 (T)	21/05/2019
ITALY	Tribunale di Milano	D.F. S.r.l. / I.C.E. S.p.A. and P.C.A. S.p.A., General Registry No. 56090	D.F. S.r.l. / I.C.E. S.p.A. and P.C.A. S.p.A., General Registry No. 56090	30/05/2019
ITALY	Tribunale di Milano	Dipharma Francis / Industria Chimica Emiliana	No. 5122	30/05/2019
ITALY	Corte d'Appello di Milano	Societa' Per Azioni Esercizi Aeroportuali / Safe Bag / Truestar Group / Aeroporti Di Roma	No. 3362/2019	30/07/2019
ITALY	Corte d'Appello di Milano	Voice plus / Eutelia / Telecom Italia	No. 3410/2019	05/08/2019
ITALY	Tribunale di Roma	CTP – Consorzio Trasporto Persone e CONCORA – Consorzio Cooperative Romane Autonoleggiatori / Società Aeroporti di Roma	No. 17014	06/09/2019
UNITED KINGDOM	Competition Appeal Tribunal	Ensign Bus Company Limited v London Southend Airport Company Limited	1331/5/7/19	03/10/2019
ITALY	Tribunale di Roma	Medov Civitavecchia / Port Mobility	No. 19637	14/10/2019
ITALY	Corte d'Appello di Milano	Sisal / GB	No.47/92/2019	03/12/2019
ITALY	Tribunale di Milano	Enter / Telecom Italia	No. 11772	18/12/2019
ITALY	Tribunale di Milano	Erregierre / Industria Chimica Emiliana / Prodotti Chimici Alimentari	No. 11893	23/12/2019

FRANCE	Cour d'appel de Paris	Google c/ LeGuide	RG 19/12553	07/01/2020
FRANCE	Cour de Cassation chambre commerciale	Sifam	No. 16-12539	15/01/2020
ITALY	Corte d'Appello di Milano	Quanta / Comune di Milano / Milanosport	No. 254	17/01/2020
ITALY	Corte d'Appello di Milano	Societa Esercizi Aeroportuali / ITR Handling	No. 222/2020	23/01/2020
ITALY	Tribunale di Roma	Digital Galaxy / Telecom Italia	No. 2063	30/01/2020
ITALY	Tribunale di Roma	P.V. / Gamenet	No. 3314	10/02/2020
ITALY	Tribunale di Roma	G.M.C. International Trade / Trenitalia	No. 4978	09/03/2020
ITALY	Tribunale ordinario di Roma	Air Bp Italia / Aeroporti Di Roma	No. 5015	10/03/2020
ITALY	Tribunale di Milano	Grifone / Pnp Italia / Studio Amministrativo Di Ornella Poetto / Com.In Service / Agenzia Delle Entrate	No. 2121	16/03/2020
UNITED KINGDOM	High Court of Justice	Infederation Ltd v Google LLC & Ors	[2020] EWHC 657 (Ch)	18/03/2020
ITALY	Corte d'Appello di Milano	Societa Esercizi Aeroportuali / UPS SCS	No.1093	14/05/2020
ITALY	Corte d'Appello di Milano	Societa Esercizi Aeroportuali / Qatar Airways	No. 1242	21/05/2020
ITALY	Tribunale di Milano	Freschi & Schiavoni / Societa' Per Azioni Esercizi Aeroportuali S.E.A.	No. 2894	21/05/2020
ITALY	Tribunale ordinario di Roma	ATS – Automazione Traffico Semafori / Faac	No. 8201	05/06/2020

ITALY	Corte d'Appello di Milano	Brussels Airlines SA/NV, American Airlines Inc. and Aegean Airlines SA / SEA S.p.A.	No. 1738	08/07/2020
ITALY	Corte d'Appello di Milano	CAD LEO ANTELLI S.R.L., AGILITY LOGISTICS S.R.L. E LATASPED S.R. / SOCIETA' PER AZIONI ESERCIZI AEROPO RTUALI S.E.A	No. 2029/2020	31/07/2020
ITALY	Tribunale di Roma	Alitalia Linee Aeree Italiane / Kuwait Petroleum Italia	No. 11474	07/08/2020
UNITED KINGDOM	Supreme Court	Huawei ZTE v. Unwired Conversant	UKSC 2019/0042	26/08/2020
ITALY	Corte d'Appello di Milano	Societa Esercizi Aeroportuali / Schenker Italiana	No. 2167	01/09/2020
ITALY	Tribunale di Milano	Schenker Italiana / S.E.A.	No. 8089	09/12/2020
ITALY	Tribunale di Milano	Lt Multimedia / Sky Italia	No. 229	14/01/2021
ITALY	Tribunale di Milano	Hirux International / J.P. Industries	No. 966	05/02/2021
FRANCE	Tribunal de Commerce Paris	Google / Oxone	RG 2020035242	10/02/2021
ITALY	Corte d'Appello di Milano	Società Esercizi Aeroportuali / Alicargo, Cad Alicargo, Carioni Sped.Ni Int. Li, De Lorenzis, Fabo Italservices, Sebi, Sigma Trans International, Ceva Freight Italy, First International & Co., Antonelli Transit Air Malpensa	No. 1097	06/04/2021

ITALY	Corte d'Appello di Milano	Vodafone / EUTELIA	No 1919	18/06/2021
ITALY	Tribunale di Milano	Metaenergia / Megareti	No. 5578	29/06/2021
ITALY	Tribunale ordinario di Milano	Vodafone Italia / Telecom Italia	No. 5757	01/07/2021
ITALY	Corte d'Appello di Milano	Societa' Per Azioni / U.S. S.R.L.	No. 2057	01/07/2021
ITALY	Tribunale di Milano	Hera Trading / Trans Austria Gasleitung	No. 6374	22/07/2021
ITALY	Corte d'Appello di Milano	Societa' Per Azioni Esercizi Aeroportuali S.E.A / Air Kosmo, Aviosped S.N.C. Di Vincenzo Barbaglia & C., Battaglino Sbc Srl Agenzia Doganale, Centro Di Assistenza Doganale Battaglino Srl, Soc. Import-Export La Minerva Di Del Prete Antonio E Guglielmo Fernando E C. Sas., "Laser S.R.L. Agenzia Doganale", Centro Di Assistenza Doganale Mollica S.R.L., Schenker Italiana Spa	No.2450	27/07/2021
ITALY	Tribunale di Milano	Logistica Mediterranea / Onorato Armatori	No. 7025	23/08/2021
ITALY	Corte d'Appello di Milano	Societa Esercizi Aeroportuali / Korean Airlines	No. 2554	02/09/2021
ITALY	Corte d'Appello di Milano	Digital World / Sky Italia	No. 2701	21/09/2021
FRANCE	Cour d'Appel de Paris	Canal + c/ LFP	RG 20/14416	24/09/2021

FRANCE	Cour de Cassation chambre commerciale	SFR / Orange	No. 14-26815	24/09/2021
ITALY	Corte d'Appello di Milano	Agroservizi / Agenzia Dell'Entrate	No. 2979	15/10/2021
ITALY	Tribunale ordinario di Milano	Absolute / Rcs Mediagroup / P Publishing	No. 9676	23/11/2021
FRANCE	Cour d'Appel de Paris	SAS IQVIA Opérations France c/ SAS Euris Health Digital Solution et SA Cegedim	RG 19/01975	08/12/2021
ITALY	Tribunale di Milano	Metaenergia / Deval	No. 701	28/01/2022
UNITED KINGDOM	Competition Appeal Tribunal	Achilles Information Limited v Network Rail Infrastructure Limited	1298/5/7/18	11/02/2022
FRANCE	Cour d'Appel de Paris	10 Médias c/ Les Éditions P. Amaury et al.	RG 19/19239	23/02/2022
FRANCE	Cour d'Appel de Paris	SAS SHB Electric c/ Schneider Electric	RG 19/19747.	09/03/2022
ITALY	Corte d'Appello di Milano	Aeroporti de Roma / Kai / Kris / Alitalia / Societa per Azioni Esercizi Aeroportualia S.E.A. / Fallimento Aeroporto S.ANNA SPA / Aeroporto di Puglia SPA	No. 981	23/03/2022
ITALY	Corte d'Appello di Milano	Tamoil Italia / Ifatalia / Alitalia / Sea Aiport Business Joint Company / Airporti di Roma	No. 988	24/03/2022
ITALY	Tribunale di Roma	Compagnia Italiana Automobili / Ford Italia	No. 5913	20/04/2022
ITALY	Tribunale ordinario di Milano	Fallimento Rs Italia / Gruppo Inox	No. 3458	20/04/2022

FRANCE	Cour d'Appel de Paris	CNAMTS c/ SA Sanofi and SA Sanofi-Aventis France	RG 19/19969	20/04/2022
UNITED KINGDOM	Competition Appeal Tribunal	Consumers' Association v Qualcomm Incorporated	1382/7/7/21	17/05/2022
ITALY	Tribunale ordinario di Roma	Metaenergia / Areti	No. 10042	22/06/2022
UNITED KINGDOM	Competition Appeal Tribunal	Justin Gutmann v First MTR South Western Trains Limited and Another & Justin Gutmann v London & South Eastern Railway Limited	1304/7/7/19	28/07/2022
ITALY	Tribunale di Milano	Codacons / Rolex Italia	No. 7389	27/09/2022
ITALY	Tribunale ordinario di Milano	Nippon Cargo Airlines / Societa' Per Azioni Esercizi Aeroportuali S.E.A	No. 8292	21/10/2022
ITALY	Tribunale ordinario di Milano	Coprem / Bonna Sabla	No. 8365	25/10/2022
ITALY	Corte d'Appello di Milano	Compagnia Italiana Di Navigazione / Logistica Mediterranea	No. 3586	14/11/2022
UNITED KINGDOM	Competition Appeal Tribunal	Home insurance consumer action limited v. BGL (holdings limited), BGL group limited, BISL limited, Compare the market limited	1423/7/7/21	09/12/2022
ITALY	Tribunale ordinario di Milano	Fallimento Agf / Adidas Italy	No. 10329	30/12/2022
FRANCE	Cour de Cassation	SA Digicel Antilles Françaises Guyave v. SA Orange et SA Orange Caraïbe	RG n°17/23041	01/03/2023

UNITED KINGDOM	Competition Appeal Tribunal	International Tin Association	1379/5/7/20	13/03/2023
UNITED KINGDOM	Competition Appeal Tribunal	Epic Games, Inc. and Others v Alphabet Inc., Google LLC and Others	1378/5/7/20	18/04/2023
UNITED KINGDOM	Court of Appeal	The Secretary of State for Health & Anor v Servier Laboratories Ltd & Ors	[2023] EWCA Civ 763	03/07/2023
UNITED KINGDOM	Competition Appeal Tribunal	Kelkoo.com (United Kingdom) Limited & Others v Google United Kingdom Limited & Other	1424/5/7/21 (T)	26/07/2023

Chapter 2
The anti-steering provision of article 5 (4) of the DMA. A law and economics assessment on the business model of gatekeepers and business users

Essay co-authored with Christian Rusche, German Economic Institute (IW). Introductory note to this chapter: this chapter was written before the first gatekeepers were designated under the DMA. *The Essay was published in the European Journal of Law & Economics: The anti-steering provision of Article 5 (4) of the DMA: a law and economics assessment on the business model of gatekeepers and business users | European Journal of Law and Economics | Springer Nature Link*

2.1 Introduction

98. A business model which has proven to be particularly successful in recent decades is the platform business model. By using digital technologies, digital platforms became more and more important and achieved unprecedented market power in a short time. According to Demary and Rusche (2018, 8), a digital platform "uses the internet to facilitate economically beneficial interactions between two or more independent groups of users." This definition has two dimensions. First, a digital platform collects and makes use of data from all user groups and involved market participants, respectively. Second, the platform provides an infrastructure for transactions and facilitates transactions between its users, i.e., the platform matches the demand and supply side and acts as a kind of gatekeeper between them. Against the backdrop of the fact that there is a competition for the market, instead of a competition on the market (Shapiro/Varian, 1999; Demary/Rusche, 2018), the platform that offers the highest effectiveness in facilitating transactions has an advantage in competition and can quickly become dominant. Data, which is key for designing and improving the matching process, is the core of the business model of the platform (Buechel et al., 2022). Along with extreme returns to scale and network externalities, the improved matching process is important for their growth and for maintaining the dominant position once achieved (Demary/Rusche, 2018; Crémer report, 2019). Since the economic importance and overall impact of platforms on society have risen in recent years (Buechel/Rusche, 2021), and there are hints that platforms distort competition (Demary/Engels/Rusche, 2020), as well as recent legal procedures[1] against platforms abusing their market power to force business users to use additional platform services, policymakers have made an increasing effort to regulate platforms and the digital economy as a whole.

99. The Digital Markets Act[2] (DMA) is one important result of the increased efforts to regulate platforms. The DMA is a sector-specific regulation which aims at setting rules "to ensure contestability and fairness for the markets in the digital sector" (Recital 7) in the EU, for both the "benefits of the business users and end users" (Article 1). The DMA targets "gatekeepers," relatively to their core platform services. The services that are core platform services are listed in Article 2 (2) of the DMA. Among others, online search engines, web browsers or cloud computing services.

1 For example, Authority for Consumers & Markets, 2022, Apple changes unfair conditions, allows alternative payments methods in dating apps, https://www.acm.nl/en/publications/acm-apple-changes-unfair-conditions-allows-alternative-payments-methods-dating-apps [Aug. 29, 2021]; European, Commission, 2021, Antitrust: Commission sends statement of objections to Apple on app store rules for music streaming providers, press release, https://ec.europa.eu/commission/presscorner/detail/en/ip_21_2061 [Aug. 29, 2022]

2 Regulation (EU) 2022/1925 of the European Parliament and of the Council of September 14, 2022 on contestable and fair markets in the digital sector and amending Directives (EU) 2019/1937 and (EU) 2020/1828 (Digital Markets Act)

The DMA was published in the Official Journal of the European Union on October 12, 2022. The DMA specifies obligations for the gatekeepers, which relate closely to major past and on-going infringement cases in regard to competition case law in digital markets (Petit, 2021). When designated, a gatekeeper should comply with all the obligations in Article 5 directly, while the obligations contained in Article 6 and Article 7 are subject to further specification.

100. This paper focusses on the fourth obligation of Art. 5 (in the following referred to as "the obligation"). Specifically, the simple game-theoretic framework adopted in this analysis illustrates how the anti-steering obligation under the DMA reshapes incentives for platforms and business users by comparing payoff structures across strategic choices. However, it does not formally derive or characterize an equilibrium outcome (e.g., a Nash equilibrium where no player has an incentive to deviate), and this remains an open element for further refinement. Hence, this paper provides a theoretical framework, with the purpose of reasoning the potential effects of the entry of the obligation. The obligation reads as follows: "The gatekeeper shall allow business users, free of charge, to communicate and promote offers, including under different conditions, to end users acquired via its core platform service or through other channels, and to conclude contracts with those end users, regardless of whether, for that purpose, they use the core platform services of the gatekeeper." This obligation was introduced to target anti-steering clauses between platforms and business users. According to the impact assessment of the DMA (European Commission, 2020, 11) a clause can be termed an anti-steering clause if business users of the gatekeeper are prevented by this clause from "directing acquired consumers to offers other than those provided on the platform, even though such alternative offers may be cheaper or otherwise potentially more attractive."

101. Several reasons triggered our interest in this obligation. First, there is very little case law on both the EU and US side, and the comparison between the EU and the US side is a striking demonstration of the difference in competition enforcement. Second, core platform services, as defined by the DMA in its Art. 2 (2), are more extensive than the market definition in competition law cases dealing with anti-steering practices. Therefore, if the platform is designated as a gatekeeper, it will have the obligation to remove anti-steering clauses from all its contracts concluded with its business users. Accordingly, the impact of the obligation is wider than case-by-case competition law. The statement of objections to Apple[3] highlights this point. While the Commission directly has to target the music streaming market and any other market where Apple might abuse its dominance in a comparable way, once designated as a gatekeeper,

3 Ibid Footnote 3

such clauses would be forbidden immediately in any core services market. Third, the impact of the obligation is also presumably more effective because of the announced fast implementation of the DMA and of the risks borne by the platform in case of noncompliance (fines up to 10% of their worldwide sales in the preceding financial year if the gatekeeper fails to comply with any of the obligations laid down in Articles 5, 6 and 7; and up to 20% when a gatekeeper has committed the same or a similar infringement (Art. 30). The short time frame and higher fines are expected to create greater overall incentives than the application of competition law. Finally, this paper builds on the potential effects of the obligation raised by the EU Commission Joint Research Center report from a panel of economic experts on the DMA. According to the economic experts, the possibility for service providers to route payments through their own websites may, for the developers, create an incentive to reduce app download prices. However, app stores being deprived of aftermarket revenues may compensate by increasing market entry prices for app uploads and reviews (Cabral et al., 2021).

102. To analyze the effects of the obligation, the relevant literature regarding platforms and related business model decisions are reviewed in Section 2. The game theory model is set up in Section 3 in order to model the situation with the new obligation. Section 4 presents the results of the analysis before Section 5 discusses the results of the analysis and gives policy recommendations based on the outcomes.

2.2 Related literature and case law

103. There is an increasing body of literature that is concerned with digital platforms and the effect of their decisions on the configuration of their business model and the likely consequences. Furthermore, there is also an increasing amount of case law relating to anti-steering. Section 2.1 concentrates on case law, while 2.2 gives an analysis of the relating economic literature.

2.2.1 Case law

104. The fourth obligation of Art. 5 of the DMA was introduced to tackle anti-steering clauses which can take several forms, from bundling to an obligation to obscure information for consumers. These steering mechanisms have been considered by the literature as a form of vertical Most Favored Nation (MFN) restraints.[4] As briefly mentioned in the introduc-

4 Colangelo, Margherita, 2019, Traditional and Platform MFN Clauses under Antitrust Law: Insights from Recent Practice, Policy International Antitrust Chronicle

tion, the obligations of the DMA were designed in light of major past or on-going case law. The anti-steering clauses were the core of the Apple case that started in the Netherlands in 2019.[5]

105. In a decision of August 24, 2021, the Authority for Consumers and Markets ordered Apple to adjust the conditions for access to the Dutch App Store to allow dating app developers to use payment systems other than the Apple's App Store Payment Processing System. The Dutch Authority for Consumers & Markets (ACM) ruled that the prohibition imposed on app developers, when agreeing to the contractual conditions package imposed by Apple, from referencing within their app any alternative payments outside the App Store was an anti-steering clause. This case was also striking since Apple remained reluctant to comply with the ACM order (Meijer/Timmerman, 2021) and accumulated penalties up to EUR 50 million,[6] after which Apple complied with the order. Another key takeaway from this case is that because of the narrow market definition, the payment rules only need to be changed for a single category of apps: dating apps. The other categories of apps are not protected by the order of the ACM.

106. At the EU level, the European Commission sent a statement of objection to Apple on its App Store rules for music providers.[7] The Commission is concerned because of the imposition of two rules. First, the mandatory use of Apple's in-app purchase system, with a 30% fee collected by apple for any purchases made through the in-app purchase (IAP) system, which would result in a raising of prices according to the Commission's investigation. Second, the anti-steering provisions which prevent app developers from informing users about alternative purchasing possibilities usually being cheaper, potentially resulting in the end users paying a higher price for their music subscription services. On February 28, 2023, the EU Commission sent a follow-up statement of objection to clarify that the Commission "does no longer take a position as to the legality of the IAP obligation for the purposes of this antitrust investigation but rather focuses on the contractual restrictions that Apple imposed on app developers which prevent them from informing iPhone and iPad users of alternative music subscription options at lower prices outside of the app and to effectively choose those."[8]

---

5 Authority for Consumers & Markets, 2022, Apple changes unfair conditions, allows alternative payments methods in dating apps, https://www.acm.nl/en/publications/acm-apple-changes-unfair-conditions-allows-alternative-payments-methods-dating-apps [Aug. 29, 2021]

6 On June 11, 2022, a press release from the ACM announced that Apple finally "changes unfair conditions, allows alternative payments in dating apps"; ACM: Apple changes unfair conditions, allows alternative payments methods in dating apps | ACM.nl (last accessed on Nov. 26, 2022)

7 EU Commission, Press release, April 30, 2021: https://ec.europa.eu/commission/presscorner/detail/en/ip_21_2061 (last accessed on June 1, 2023)

8 EU Commission, Press release, February 28, 2023: https://ec.europa.eu/commission/presscorner/detail/en/ip_23_1217 (last accessed on June 1, 2023)

107. Back to the Member States level, there has been a promising effort to tackle anti-steering clauses in France. In 2017, the Minister of Economy and Finance introduced legal proceedings against Apple on the grounds of restrictive practices (which is a French specificity, Art. L.442-6 of the Commerce Code). The Minister considered that some clauses in the adhesion contract between developers and the platform contained significant imbalances in the rights and obligations for both parties. Among the clauses raised by the Minister as infringing Art. L.442-6: the exclusivity of the payment system, the 30% proportional fee and the deferred payment of amounts due to the developers (the remaining 70%). The Minister requested the immediate termination of the clauses as well as the imposition of a fine for EUR 2 million. On December 19, 2022, the Tribunal de commerce de Paris ruled that the leading position of Apple is indisputable and that the relationships between developers and the platform are economically imbalanced. However, the judges considered that the payment system exclusivity does not mean that developers are totally dependent on it, only those who have opted for the in-app purchases are dependent. According to the judges, the proportional 30% fee is not clearly excessive and is often found in online trade agreements or in brick-and-mortar stores. Interestingly, the decision from the Tribunal de commerce de Paris refers to the upcoming enforcement of the DMA, without prejudice to Apple's status as a gatekeeper.

108. It also seems relevant to mention two cases from the United States of America (US) to grasp the broader picture of the anticompetitive concerns of anti-steering clauses imposed by platforms. First, the Amex case, in the credit card market which started following the introduction of a complaint in 2010 filed by the Department of Justice and seventeen states against three bank card companies. The three bank card companies were accused of hindering competition by preventing merchants from encouraging consumers to use credit cards which offer lower operating costs for the merchants. This was an anti-steering clause. One year after the introduction of the antitrust complaint, Visa and Mastercard settled their case and removed the clauses from their contracts with their merchants. However, Amex refused to remove the clauses. Finally, on June 25, 2018, the US Supreme Court confirmed the approach of the Appeal Court on the delimitation of the relevant market, convinced by the presence of indirect network effects. The Court relied on Filistrucchi research (2014) in his reasoning on the market definition in two-sided markets. Chaiehloudj (2018) criticized the decision of the Supreme Court regarding the market definition and therefore wrongly allocating the burden of proof. The second case in the US is Epic Games vs. Apple. Epic, creator of the video game Fortnite, added its own direct payment processing option for in-app purchases made by users on the App Store, offering a 20% discount on the in-app purchase price (Chaiehloudj, 2021). However, Apple, per contract clauses requires

all in-app purchases to use the Apple's own in-app purchase system, charging a 30% commission on app developers and restricting them from informing users of possible purchasing alternatives (which constituted here the anti-steering provisions). Therefore, Apple removed Fortnite from the App Store on the grounds that Epic Games breached their contract. Epic claimed in the US District Court of California that the exclusivity and the anti-steering provisions consist of maintenance of a monopoly and denial of essential facility, constituting both an unreasonable restraint of trade and tying practices. While Apple tried to justify the anti-steering clause by relying on the Amex case, the Californian Court distinguished the two cases because Apple's anti-steering provisions prevented informed choice among users on the platform. The decision emphasized the importance of transparency and open flow of information in technology markets to avoid information costs causing lock-in effects for platforms (McMahon, 2022). The 9th U.S. Circuit Court of Appeals in April 2023 was indeed convinced that Apple uses anti-steering clauses which are an infringement of California's unfair competition law. The appeals court ordered: The offering of additional payment methods off-Apple and means for steering consumers to them for all app developers instead of just for Epic (Reuters, 2023; Supreme Court of the United States, 2023) opened a second line of conflict. Because this change for all developers implies a severe impact on this business model for Apple, which was given 90 days to pursue an appeal at the Supreme Court to avoid this. While Apple was preparing this appeal, Epic applicated at the Supreme Court for the remedies ordered to become effective in July 2023. This, however, was denied on August 9, 2023 (Supreme Court, 2023). While the remedies would not only apply to Epic, but to all app developers on the App Store, Epic still lost this legal battle, and could not get Apple sanctioned under U.S. Antitrust law for the excessive fees imposed on the app developers. To this day, Epic is still not available on the App Store.

2.3 Economic literature

109. The fourth obligation of Art. 5 of the DMA, against this backdrop, can be interpreted as prescribing some form of mixed bundling to the platform. Before this obligation, the business users were often contractually obliged to use the platform's services, for example, communication, identification, promotion and payment, for transactions with the consumer matched by the platform. There was bundling because the additional services were tied to the initial transaction. With the new obligation, the business users have the possibility to communicate and promote offers to their end-users without being prevented through contractual clauses between the business users and the platform.

110. Choi (2007), and Rochet and Tirole (2008), among others, analyzed tying, and bundling was analyzed by Sun (2018) and Lin et al. (2020), for example. Mandrescu (2021, 2) vividly described the difference between both strategies. Accordingly, tying occurs if the provision of one product or service by a company is dependent on the usage of a different product or service of the same enterprise. Bundling, however, is a special form of tying, where both products or services must be purchased together.

111. Whinston (1990) analyzes conventional markets and shows that tying is used by a firm with a monopoly in one market to deter entry into a second market with competition. Bundling, therefore, reduces the equilibrium profits of all companies. In platform markets, however, the picture is not as clear. Sun (2018) shows that bundling enhances overall welfare because it improves the internalization of indirect network effects. Lin et al. (2020) show that mixed bundling can be beneficial for the competing platforms. Among others, Luo et al. (2017) and Prasad, Venkatesh, and Mahajan (2010) reveal that network effects induce bundling strategies.

112. Following the results of Lin et al. (2020), mixed bundling can be beneficial for the platform. However, the obligation in Art. 5 (4) is specifically targeting anti-steering provisions and not bundling practices in general that are prohibited by Art. 5 (7) and Art. 5 (8) of the DMA. In practice, this is not an issue since all obligations laid down in Art. 5 are applicable when a firm is designated as a gatekeeper.

113. This paper mainly analyzes the consequences of the obligation for the business users and their decision on a business model, which was, to the best of our knowledge, off-focus in the literature on platforms so far. One exception is the paper by Kraemer, Schnurr and Wohlfarth (2019). Concerning the usage of platform services, they emphasize that using the services of the platform can be beneficial for business users in the short run but can have negative consequences in the long run because the platform can collect and make use of more data. The business user has less data because the data intensive services are done by the platform.

114. The importance of data for businesses has grown over the years (Auer et al., 2016, p. 10). Beginning in the 1960s, data was just the result of a business process. Later data became the enabler of internal processes of companies. Since 2000 it also became an enabler of products and services offered by companies. In recent years, data also became a product itself. These four different roles can be filled by the same set of data at the same time. Especially for digital platforms, data has developed into the core of the business model (Buechel et al., 2022) and one important success factor. Due to the different roles of data, data can have a positive impact on a company in different ways (for example, Demary et al., 2019, pp. 25; Buchholtz/Bukowski/Śniegocki, 2014):

- Data-to-information: Valuable information can be deduced from data.

- Data-to-product/service: Based on data, new products or services are developed or existing products or services are improved.
- Data-to-management: Data is used for better decisions in the managerial or organizational processes of enterprises, or new management or organizational processes are developed.

115. For a comprehensive overview of the economic literature studying the impact of data in digital markets, Pino (2022) carried out a survey extracting general insights, distinguishing between three classes of models according to the data collection model: data acquisition with no strategic interactions, data from consumers and data from intermediaries.

2.4 Model

2.4.1 Baseline model

116. The market can be described rather simply by using a model based on Hotelling (1929). Several authors already relied on the Hotelling model while modeling firms' interactions in two-sided markets (Spulber, 1999; Alexandrov et al., 2011). Even closer to our paper, Decarolis and Li (2023) study the Google android case. The authors identified three dimensions of the DMA and rely on a Hotelling model to demonstrate how the enforcement of these dimensions can result in a greater impact in the online search engine markets, increasing the number of potential users of competing search engines. The usage of this well-known model allows one to concentrate more on the business model decision of the platform and the business users against the backdrop of their specific groups of customers. In our paper we aim to model the strategic interaction between platforms and business users after the introduction of the anti-steering obligation. While our framework captures key shifts in incentives induced by the anti-steering obligation and illustrates comparative payoffs across strategic choices, it does not attempt to derive a complete equilibrium characterization, leaving formal equilibrium computation to future elaboration.

117. Accordingly, the consumers interested in purchasing an arbitrary good from a representative seller are independently and identically distributed on the interval $[0,1]$. Every consumer wants to purchase one unit of the good. The good is available on a platform where multiple sellers are active or in the web shop of a specific seller, i.e., they want to avoid the platform. The consumer $\alpha_P \in (0,1)$ is indifferent with regard to using the platform or using the shop of a specific seller if prices are equal. Every consumer $\alpha < \alpha_P$, with $\alpha \in [0,1)$, is using the platform and the consumers with $\alpha_P < \alpha$ are avoiding the platform and are using the web shop of a specific seller for their purchase. Because of network effects, the platform attracts more consumers, i.e., $\alpha_P \gg \frac{1}{2}$. The consumers $(0 \leq \alpha < \alpha_P)$ are prone to use a

platform either because they like the offered services or they first started to buy on this platform and, having an account with an independent seller, which is supposed to come with switching cost (Klemperer, 1987), is not worthwhile to them.

118. The consumers $\alpha_P < \alpha \leq 1$ are more prone to independent sellers or already have an account there and don't want to switch. The distance between the respective consumer and the position of the business model, furthermore, also increases the cost for the consumer, as incorporated by Hotelling (1929) as transportation cost. A consumer close to zero is completely satisfied by the services offered by the platform, while consumers close to 1 are completely satisfied by the web shop of an independent seller. The consumer $\alpha < \alpha_P$ is indifferent with regards to a web shop or the platform. Because the platform has several business users resulting in more products, and the platform has improved its services as well as the matching process, it is assumed that $\alpha_P \gg \frac{1}{2}$. The position of α_P crucially depends on the services offered and the assortment of products. For example, if the platform offers payment services that are as convenient as possible, like the famous 1-click ordering at Amazon, more consumers will stay with the platform or will use it, because this translates as low transportation cost and a higher α_P in our model. But if the platform doesn't have such a service and the consumers have to go to the business user they chose on the platform to pay for their purchases, more consumers will go directly to the web shops in the first place and stay with the web shop once directed to them by the platform because they then have an account there.

119. Furthermore, assume for the sake of simplicity that the share of demand that is not using the platform is equally divided between the business users running a web shop. The number of these web shops is denoted by $m > 0$. Hence, the specific demand of each web shop is given by $\frac{1}{m}(1 - \alpha_P)$.

120. A representative seller i has the options of only selling the good via its own shop, only selling via the platform or using both channels. For establishing and maintaining his own shop, the cost of $C_{Ci} > 0$ must be incurred by the seller. For listing his good on the platform and for being in line with the standards of the platform, costs of $\theta_i > 0$ must be paid. C_{Ci} and θ_i comprise fixed and variable elements and represent the present value of the cost of the respective business model decision. These costs are indexed by i, i.e., the costs for setting up a web shop and being compliant with the standards of the platform differ between the sellers. It is also assumed that it is more costly to run an independent web shop, i.e., $C_{Ci} > \theta_i$. For example, with an independent web shop, a business user needs a domain; the website must be programmed and hosted; investments in marketing are necessary to attract consumers; cyber security and data protection must be guaranteed; a payment system must be implemented;

and generally more resources are needed for customer relations than when a platform is used. If a platform is used, these costs are to a large extent borne by the platform. Because of economies of scale for the platform business models (Demary/Rusche, 2018) and the fees collected, the burden for every business user is rather low.

121. To facilitate analysis, the median seller is analyzed in the following. Half of the sellers must incur higher costs to establish a web shop and to be compliant, respectively, and the other roughly 50% of the sellers have lower cost.

122. The respective costs are independently and identically distributed on the interval $[C_{Min};C_{Max}]$, where $C_{Min} > 0$. The costs for the median seller are denoted by C_C and θ.

123. Furthermore, a share of C_P of the sales generated via the platform must be paid as a fee to the platform by the seller if he uses the platform. Not using the platform results in a share of $\frac{1}{m}(1-\alpha_P)$ customers using the web shop of the seller for their purchases. Accordingly, it is assumed that there is a positive number of consumers as an addressable market for the web shop of the seller. This addressable market is equal to total demand for the seller if he doesn't use the platform. In case he also uses the platform, his demand is given by $\frac{1}{m}(1-\alpha_P)+\frac{1}{n}\alpha_P$, where n denotes the number of sellers on the platform (including the seller at hand). If only the platform is used, demand is given by $\frac{1}{n}\alpha_P$. The rationale behind this assumption is that due to the uniform presentation on the platform, the number of consumers using the platform for shopping are equally divided between the active sellers. Note that this also includes the case of the platform itself acting as a seller on the platform. However, this also requires the absence of differentiated treatment by the platform, especially favoring its own products. Against this backdrop, the DMA also establishes obligations that are designed to prevent self-preferencing. Art. 6 (5), for example, forbids, if this obligation is imposed, that the platform favors its own products or services in rankings.

124. However, there are variable cost of $C_S \geq 0$ for selling one unit of the good. The price of the good is denoted by $p > 0$ and is supposed to be the same on the platform and on the possible web shop of a seller. The rationale behind this assumption is that the seller of the web shop acts as a price taker and adjusts to the price on the platform, where supply and demand of the good are sufficiently large in order to create an equilibrium price for the good. Accordingly, if the seller charges a lower price, he loses profit, while he loses customers if he charges a higher price than p. The payoffs of the median seller dependent on his choice of sale's channel are shown in Figure 1.

125. Given that the gross margin of the sale of one unit on the platform, $NP_P = (p(1 - C_P) - C_S)$, is non-negative, the platform is used if $\alpha_P NP_P > n\theta$, which follows from the condition that the profit of the activity on the platform is positive. Accordingly, if the maximum profit that can be earned on the platform is larger than the sum of total adjustment cost to the platform, the platform is used. Furthermore, if the demand that can be targeted via the platform (α_P) is large, the platform can reduce the gross margin of a seller by increasing the fee, C_P, and still being attractive to a seller. Accordingly, the platform can use a price of zero or a subsidized price for the services offered to consumers in order to attract more users or win the competition for the market in the first place, and then increase prices in order to generate profits (Sun et al., 2018). The platform can, furthermore, increase its attractiveness if the platform is designed in order to allow easy adjustment to the standards of the platform (low θ).

Figure 1: Payoffs of the median seller dependent on the channel(s) he uses

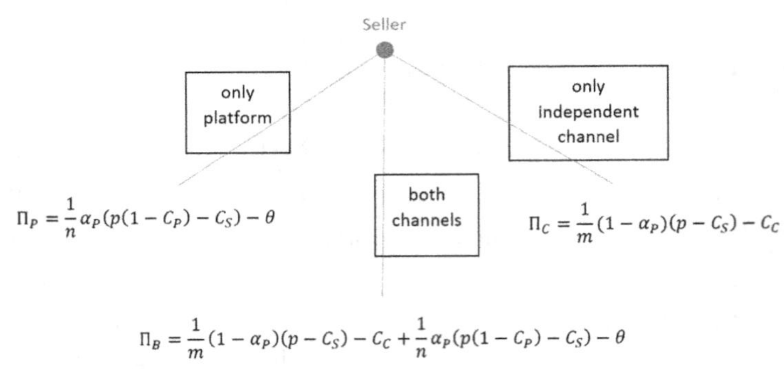

Source: Author's depiction

126. If the gross margin for the sale of one unit on the web shop NP_C is positive, i.e., $p - C_S > 0$, the web shop is used if $(1 - \alpha_P)NP_C > mC_C$. Note that due to the fee for sales on the platform, if the gross margin on the platform NP_P is positive, NP_C is also positive. Accordingly, selling one additional unit in the independent web shop is more attractive than selling the same unit on the platform. However, the cost advantage and the additional users that can be served by using a platform can induce the (sole) usage of a platform.

127. In the baseline model, it holds that for the serving of customers on the platform only the platform services can be used. From the perspective of the seller, the customers that can be targeted with the web shop and the customers that can be targeted by using the platform form two separate markets. In the following, the new obligation of the DMA is introduced to relax this assumption.

2.4.2 Baseline model with new obligation

128. The assumptions of the baseline model in 3.1 still hold except that the share α_P of the consumers that are active on the platform can be divided into $\alpha_P = \alpha'_P + \alpha_{PS}$. $\alpha_{PS} > 0$ denotes the share of platform users that are prone to purchasing the good in a web shop if the seller addresses them using promotions, etc. over the channels of the platform or other channels. The number of sellers applying such promotions is given by $k < n$. Accordingly, the use of the new obligation by some sellers reduces the addressable market to the sellers that only use the platform because only the share $\alpha'_P < \alpha_P$ of users can be targeted by using the channels of the platform.

129. If only the independent channel is used, the payoff Π_C is unchanged compared to the baseline model. If the seller only sells via the platform, his addressable market is now α'_P. Since there are $(n-1)$ other sellers competing for the customers, the number of customers served is given by $\frac{1}{n}\alpha'_P$. It is assumed that the fee charged by the platform, and hence the gross margin on the platform per unit, is unchanged compared to the baseline model. Accordingly, the payoff of the seller can be denoted by $\Pi_P = \frac{1}{n}\alpha'_P NP_P - \theta$.

130. It is further assumed that the opportunity to serve customers from the platform can only be used if there is an independent channel, i.e., the seller has an independent web shop. Accordingly, it is assumed that there are some professional channels established by the seller that can be used if a web shop exists. This assumption also excludes private sellers, for example on eBay, in the analysis, in order to set a focus on business users as in the obligation of the DMA. It is also assumed that the cost of targeting and serving the customers of the platform with independent channels are negligible because the processes and capabilities are already established by the setting up of the web shop (C_C) and the adoption to the platform (θ), respectively.

131. In essence, the number of customers served by the independent web shop is given by $\left(\frac{1}{m}(1-\alpha_P) + \frac{1}{k}\alpha_{PS}\right)$ if both channels and the opportunities of the obligation are used. $\frac{1}{m}(1-\alpha_P)$ are the customers that have already used the web shop of the seller and $\frac{1}{k}\alpha_{PS}$ are the customers that were redirected from the platform. The gross margin earned with each unit sold on the web shop is NP_C. $\frac{1}{n}\alpha'_P$ are the customers served by using the channels of the platform. The gross margin per unit for these sales is NP_P. Accordingly, the profit is given by $\Pi_B = \left(\frac{1}{m}(1-\alpha_P) + \frac{1}{k}\alpha_{PS}\right)NP_C - C_C + \frac{1}{n}\alpha'_P NP_P - \theta$.

2.4.3 Baseline model with new obligation and economic benefits of data

132. Regarding the model of the paper, data can be used to increase the sales or turnover (data-to-information), decrease the cost of the independent channel or the cost of using the platform (data-to-management), and decrease the cost of sales or increase the price that can be charged due to better products/services (data-to-product/service). To internalize the benefits of data into the model, the function $\tau(D)$ is added to the payoff, where D represents the amount of data available or that is used for analysis, respectively. This approach is used to include any benefit that can be generated using data in the model. The effect is a net effect, that means τ gives the benefits of data after subtracting the cost for obtaining these benefits, for example, the cost for generating, saving or analyzing data. It is assumed that $\tau(0) = 0$, which means, if no data is available or no data is used, data exhibits no benefit for the company. The benefits of data for the companies are strictly increasing with the amount of data, i.e., $\tau' > 0$, but at a decreasing rate, i.e., $\tau'' < 0$. These assumptions are based on the findings of Moody/Walsh (1999) in their analysis of information. Furthermore, it is assumed that the platform can deduce more valuable information from a similar amount of data than any other enterprise, because data and, therefore, the analysis of data are the core of the business model of a digital platform: For a similar amount of data ($\bar{D}$), the platform (*Plattform*) can generate a greater benefit than any other arbitrary enterprise (E), i.e., $\overline{\tau}_{Plattform}(\bar{D}) > \overline{\tau}_E(\bar{D})$. The resulting payoffs for the seller based on the business model used are given in Figure 2. Note that the baseline models with and without the obligation are a specific case of the model with the benefits of data ($\tau(0) = 0$).

133. The amount of data available is approximated by the number of transactions that are processed by the platform or the seller, respectively. Since every consumer only buys one unit, the number of transactions in the model is equal to the number of customers served and the number of units sold. That means, more transactions lead to the generation of more data, yielding a higher return from the analysis of data. In our model the maximum number of consumers is restricted. Nevertheless, if the assumption is loosened, the data can be used to attract more consumers, which then result in more data and so forth. I.e., a self-reinforcing growth process similar to reinforcing positive indirect network effects can be started (Demary and Rusche, 2018). In the model with the new obligation, if the seller uses both channels, he has access to data of the transactions done in his own web shop $\left(\frac{1}{m}(1-\alpha_P)+\frac{1}{k}\alpha_{PS}\right)$ and the transactions on the platform $\left(\frac{1}{n}\alpha'_P\right)$.

134. Accordingly, it is assumed that the business users indeed make use of the data that can be collected, although there is evidence that so far not all companies make use of the opportunities offered by their data (Buechel and Engels, 2022).

Figure 2: Payoffs of the median seller dependent on the channel(s) he uses with the new obligation and the benefits of data

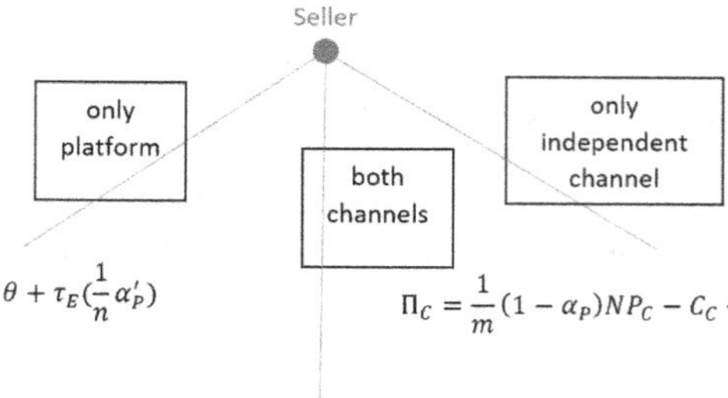

$$\Pi_P = \frac{1}{n}\alpha'_P NP_P - \theta + \tau_E(\frac{1}{n}\alpha'_P)$$

$$\Pi_C = \frac{1}{m}(1-\alpha_P)NP_C - C_C + \tau_E(\frac{1}{m}(1-\alpha_P))$$

$$\Pi_B = \left(\frac{1}{m}(1-\alpha_P) + \frac{1}{k}\alpha_{PS}\right)NP_C - C_C + \frac{1}{n}\alpha'_P NP_P - \theta + \tau_E(\frac{1}{m}(1-\alpha_P) + \frac{1}{k}\alpha_{PS} + \frac{1}{n}\alpha'_P)$$

Source: Author's depiction

2.4.4 Payoff and data of the platform

135. The question arises: What amount of data does the platform have access to? It is unchallenged that the platform has access to the data that can be generated from the transactions facilitated and processed by the platform (α'_P). In this article, it is assumed that the platform can also learn something from the share of the demand α_{PS} that was diverted to the web shops of the business users. First, these customers were, at least to some extent, targeted by using the channels of the platform and, therefore, the platform can gain some insights. Secondly, the platform has access to the data collected before the obligation was introduced/enforced. A comparison between the data before the new obligation and the data collected after the introduction of the obligation can yield further insights, especially on the characteristics of the users that left – and how they can be targeted and reclaimed by the platform. Especially, because they still have an account on the platform, which makes it likely that they will use it again in the future. Additionally, the platform can potentially also access the data from the customers of a seller that are served by using the services of the platform.

136. Furthermore, the amount of data the platform can collect and analyze is also dependent on the number of business users. This also follows from the platform business model that concentrates on matching users from the different markets/user groups (Buechel et al., 2022). When a business user joins the platform and provides the respective information, for example, on the type and quantity of products offered, as well as the reaction of

consumers to the new seller, the platform can gain interesting insights. To include this into the model, the benefits of data for the platform are also dependent on the number of business users n. Note that the benefits of data for a business user are also dependent on the number of platforms it uses. Because we are assuming only one platform, the information is the same for the business users and, therefore, not considered separately. This even holds for non-platform users because they can analyze the data available on the most important platform.

137. The resulting payoffs of the platform are given by the benefits generated based on the data that it collected and the fees for the facilitated transactions between its users. In the model with the obligation and the benefits of data, the payoff of the platform Π^P is given by: $\Pi^P = \alpha'_P C_P + \tau_P(\alpha'_P + \alpha_{PS}, n) - F_P$. F_P denote the fixed cost of the platform for establishing the platform. It is assumed that the variable cost of the platform is zero due to the economies of scale for digital platforms. This assumption also includes that the platform is not active as a seller on the platform. The consequence of relaxing this assumption is addressed in Section 4. It is furthermore assumed that at least one business user uses the new obligation and, therefore, some consumers are diverted to the independent web shop. θ is not included in the payoffs of the platform because these are the costs the business users must incur in order to be compliant with the standards of the platform, which is the prerequisite for using the platform. These costs are necessary for adopting the standards and don't represent a flow of payments to the platform or a service offered by the platform.

138. For the moment, it is also assumed that C_P is not changed by the platform. An increase by the platform would initially lead to higher profits for the platform, but a second effect is that being active on the platform becomes unattractive to at least some of the business users, which limits the choices for consumers, the data that is collected and, because of both, also the fees earned. Nevertheless, Section 4 analyzes the consequences that the new obligation and, therefore, the decisions of the business users have on the decision of the platform in regards to the share of the sales charged as a fee.

2.5 Business model decision

2.5.1 Joining the platform

139. The reaction to the new obligation by business users will also determine the reaction(s) of the platform. If the business users use the new obligation to divert consumer payments away from the platform, this has consequences on the payoff of the platform, which may cause a reaction by the platform. Accordingly, the choice of business users is analyzed in

the following subsection. This also allows for an analysis of the situation of the platform afterwards.

140. If the benefits due to data are left aside for the moment, the following holds:

Proposition 1: Following the introduction of the new obligation, business users with an independent web shop will have an increased incentive to also join the platform, and business users that only used the platform will be more likely to establish an independent web shop, and once both channels are used, the new obligation will be relied upon.

Proof: To prove the proposition, three things regarding the median business user must be shown:

1. Once both channels are used, the new obligation will be relied upon to address some customers.
2. Business users that only used their independent web shop will now have an increased incentive to join the platform.
3. Business users that only used the platform will be more likely to establish an independent web shop.

(1) The profit for the median business user if both channels and the obligation are used is given by

$\Pi_B = \left(\frac{1}{m}(1-\alpha_P) + \frac{1}{k}\alpha_{PS}\right)NP_C - C_C + \frac{1}{n}\alpha_P' NP_P - \theta$ (Section 3.2).

The payoff without applying the obligation with both channels is $\Pi_B^0 = \frac{1}{m}(1-\alpha_P)NP_C - C_C + \frac{1}{n}\alpha_P' NP_P - \theta.$

$\Pi_B > \Pi_B^0$ holds, if $\frac{1}{k}\alpha_{PS}NP_C > 0$. The new obligation leads to a reduction of the addressable market on the platform because some of the consumers are targeted and served by competitors. The new obligation, however, offers the opportunity to attract some additional users, and this opportunity is seized by the business users. The gross margin per unit of the independent web shop (NP_C) is positive. This follows from the usage of the platform, where the gross margin (NP_P) is lower than NP_C due to the fee charged by the platform. Because $NP_C > 0$, it is fruitful to also use the new obligation to acquire some users that are prone to deal with business users off the platform. This assumes that the cost for contacting the users is included in the fixed cost of the independent channel and the cost spent on becoming compliant with the standards of the platform, and the exact wording "free of charge" laid down in the obligation. On the basis of this, the following can be deduced for the rest of the article:

Lemma 1: Every business user with an independent web shop will try to acquire some consumers on the platform, that means $k = n$, once this opportunity is offered free of charge.

Note that this also holds for the platform itself. The platform is the web shop of the vertically integrated platform company. Being aware that the business users are targeting the consumers, the platform can also target the consumers in order to increase sales and decrease the loss because of diverted consumers. The gross margin per unit of sales of the platform company on its own platform is assumed to be NP_C because the cost of the fees is internalized by the platform.

(2) The profit for the median business user if he only uses his independent web shop is given by

$\Pi_C = \frac{1}{m}(1-\alpha_P)NP_C - C_C$. The profit with an additional shop on the platform is given by

$\Pi_B = \left(\frac{1}{m}(1-\alpha_P) + \frac{1}{k}\alpha_{PS}\right)NP_C - C_C + \frac{1}{n}\alpha'_P NP_P - \theta$. Due to the joining of the platform in this situation, additional sales of

$\Pi_B - \Pi_C = \Pi_{Diff2} = \left(\frac{1}{k}\alpha_{PS}\right)NP_C + \frac{1}{n}\alpha'_P NP_P - \theta$ can be generated. Using the result of lemma 1, it produces $\Pi_{Diff2} = \left(\frac{1}{n}\alpha_{PS}\right)NP_C + \frac{1}{n}\alpha'_P NP_P - \theta$.

Without the obligation, this additional revenue is given by $\Pi_{Diff1} = \frac{1}{n}\alpha_P NP_P - \theta$. The additional sales, in both cases, determine whether the platform is used or not. If the additional sales are at least zero, the platform is used. It holds, however, that the additional sales with the new obligation are greater than the additional sales without the obligation. That means, the obligation, indeed, makes it more profitable for the median business user to actually use the platform. This is since $\Pi_{Diff2} > \Pi_{Diff1}$. This is given if $\left(\frac{1}{n}\alpha_{PS}\right)NP_C + \frac{1}{n}\alpha'_P NP_P - \theta > \frac{1}{n}\alpha_P NP_P - \theta$.

Because it holds that $\alpha_P = \alpha_{PS} + \alpha'_P$, and, due to canceling out similar terms, this reduces to

$$NP_C > NP_P.$$

As mentioned in (1), the gross margin on the platform is supposed to be lower than the gross margin per unit in the web shop of the seller because of the fee charged by the platform for facilitating the respective transaction. If this indeed holds, the new obligation makes it more attractive for business users with a web shop to join the platform. This is true for the median seller and every other seller because the increased incentive is independent of the specific cost of joining the platform. Joining the platform is more attractive as long as the margin in the independent web shop is higher because the obligation allows for increasing the sales of the web shop. Furthermore, the sales are also increased due to sales on the platform. Without the obligation, however, only the additional sales on the platform, where the gross margin per unit is supposed to be lower than in the web shop, worked as an incentive for joining the platform. Accordingly, the new obligation likely increases the number of business users on the platform. The term "likely" is used because it is not necessarily the case that the number of business users rises. For example, if using the platform was attractive before, i.e., the specific costs for a business user to join the platform are sufficiently low, the new obligation, although even increasing the attractiveness, does not lead to an increase in the number of business users. And although every business user already uses the platform, the greater attractiveness may also increase the opportunities of the platform to raise fees, for example. Nevertheless, if the usage of the platform was not attractive before, the introduction of the new obligation may have changed this.

(3) The payoff for the median business user that is only using the platform before the obligation is $\Pi_P = \frac{1}{n}\alpha_P NP_P - \theta$. After introduction, this payoff falls to $\Pi_P = \frac{1}{n}\alpha'_P NP_P - \theta$ if it is assumed, for the moment, that the number of business users on the platform remains constant. Accordingly, now, the number of potential customers is reduced because some of the customers were diverted away from the platform by other business users ($\alpha_P > \alpha'_P$). By establishing an independent web shop, the business user can win back some of these customers and serve additional customers with the web shop at a higher gross margin. The additional sales of the web shop are $\Pi_{Diff3} = \left(\frac{1}{m}(1-\alpha_P) + \frac{1}{n}\alpha_{PS}\right)NP_C - C_C$ with the new obligation. Without the obligation the additional sales are $\Pi_{Diff4} = \frac{1}{m}(1-\alpha_P)NP_C - C_C$. The additional sales with the new obligation Π_{Diff3} are larger than Π_{Diff4} for the median seller and for every other seller, assuming the number of web shops before and after the obligation being the same, for the moment. This is due to the additional users that come from the platform and can be served at a higher gross margin per unit, while the cost for establishing the web shop is the same. The non-platform users that can be served with the web shop is also supposed to be the same with or without the new obligation for a business user that had no web shop before. Due to the higher additional sales of the web shop, it becomes more likely that pure platform business users will start their own web shop. However, the absolute number of business users must not necessarily increase. For example, if all platform users had a web shop before, the increased additional sales will not lead to additional web shops.

141. In essence, the new obligation will cause business users to target the customers on the platform. Even business users without a web shop might establish a web shop in order to attract new users and divert some of the customers from the platform. Furthermore, if all business users have not

already joined the platform, it is more likely that they will do so. The change in incentive is analyzed here in order to show the consequences on the business model decision of the business user. Whether or not a specific business model decision is made or not, crucially depends, among other factors, on the specific costs.

142. Nevertheless, since the number of business users of the platform is likely to increase, competition on the platform and competition for the diverted customers of the platform also probably becomes more severe. The increased competition can then decrease the incentives to additionally use the platform. However, the decreased incentives come into play when the number of business users has already increased. Accordingly, the number of business users is supposed to be higher with the obligation than without the obligation if the number before and after the introduction of the obligation is constant.

143. Nevertheless, the incentives to join the platform even with an increased number of competitors is higher with the obligation if the following holds:

$$\frac{1}{n'}\alpha_{PS}NP_C + \frac{1}{n'}\alpha'_P NP_P - \theta > \frac{1}{n}\alpha_P NP_P - \theta .$$

144. Applying $n' = n + x$, where $x \geq 0$ denotes the number of additional business users on the platform, and $NP_C = NP_P + pC_P$, which is the difference between the gross margin on the web shop and on the platform, yields:

$$\alpha_{PS} pC_P > \frac{x}{n}\alpha_P NP_P .$$

145. The left-hand side represents the saved payments to the platform because some customers are served using the web shop. The right-hand side represents the sales from the platform customers that are served by new competitors. This result implies that the incentive to join the platform is positive if the number of new competitors is zero or close to zero, while the number of competitors on the platform is already high. Furthermore, if the gross margin per unit sold on the platform is zero – which makes it unattractive to join the platform in the baseline model – joining the platform may even become attractive under such circumstances due to the obligation because this decision allows for selling some additional units to platform users at a higher margin on the web shop. This result is also independent of the cost of joining the platform for a specific user, because just the difference in payoffs is considered for the business model decision. The costs, however, are supposed to be unaffected by the obligation. In essence, as mentioned earlier:

Proposition 2: The new obligation will lead to an increased incentive for business users to use the platform as long as they weren't using the platform anyways. This especially holds without the benefits that can be realized by making use of data generated with the transactions.

2.5.2 Starting an independent web shop

146. In terms of the decision by platform business users to start an independent web shop or not, it holds that as long as the number of web shops is unchanged, then establishing an independent web shop becomes more attractive after the introduction of the new obligation as long as the following, which is analogous to the analysis in (3) in the proof of Proposition 1, holds:

$$\frac{1}{n'}\alpha_{PS}NP_C > 0.$$

147. Accordingly, even with stiffer competition on the platform, establishing a web shop becomes more attractive. On the one hand, the web shop is a way to establish a second sales channel to limit the reduction in sales because of competition. On the other hand, the independent web shop is a means to react to competitors by targeting new or old users that can be served in the independent web shop at a higher margin. Nevertheless, since the incentive to establish a web shop increases, the number of web shops and, therefore, competition off the platform is also likely to increase.

148. To analyze this situation, suppose that the number of web shops initially increases to $m' - 1 \geq m - 1$ due to the obligation. The median business user is then confronted with the decision of whether to become the owner of web shop no. m' or not. Once the web shop is established, the number of web shops increases accordingly; otherwise, it stays unchanged. Although competition on and off the platform becomes more severe, the incentives to establish an independent web shop increase if the following holds:

$$\frac{1}{n'}\alpha_{PS} > \left(\frac{1}{m} - \frac{1}{m'}\right)(1 - \alpha_P).$$

149. Note that this concentrates on the change in incentives for establishing a web shop. On the left-hand side is given the additional share of demand from the platform that can be served with the independent web shop. Since the opportunity of diverting platform customers is new, this comprises all the customers that can be acquired this way. The right-hand side gives the reduction of individual demand for every owner of a web shop that was caused by the increased competition following the introduction of the obligation. Because there was the opportunity to serve new customers with the web shop before, only the change in expected demand is considered. Furthermore, this inequation is independent of the gross margin and the specific cost at hand. As a consequence, therefore, the introduction of the obligation, which is meant to open new opportunities for business users, may even hurt them due to more intense competition. This is the case when the additional competition between the web shops causes a higher drop in demand than what can be targeted from the platform. However, if m and m' are sufficiently large, this difference is close to zero and, therefore, establishing a web shop becomes more attractive because

the new opportunity of targeting platform markets. This also holds if only a very small share of total demand is off-platform demand.

150. In the model it is assumed that the total number of consumers is constant. The increased attractiveness of the platform due to more sellers and, hence, more choice and the new web shops off the platform, however, can also lead to more consumers shopping online. This implies that the negative effects of more competition are mitigated. Consequently, the results of Proposition 1 are confirmed. A possible additional effect of the obligation, hence, is the encouraged usage of e-commerce. The analysis of this, however, is left for future research.

2.5.3 The effect of data

151. The introduction of data into the analysis reveals that the results of Proposition 1 still hold. Accordingly, the obligation will be used (1), business users with a shop on a platform will also be more likely to establish an independent web shop (2), and business users that only have a web shop will also be more likely to join the platform (a higher probability) (3). This result follows from the assumption that the marginal utility of data is positive. Accordingly, if sales are increased, more data is available for analysis, which then leads to greater benefits that can be realized.

(1) The payoff with the new obligation if both channels and the obligation are used is given by

$$\Pi_B^D = \left(\frac{1}{m}(1-\alpha_P) + \frac{1}{k}\alpha_{PS}\right)NP_C - C_C + \frac{1}{n}\alpha'_P NP_P - \theta$$
$$+ \tau_E\left(\frac{1}{m}(1-\alpha_P) + \frac{1}{k}\alpha_{PS} + \frac{1}{n}\alpha'_P\right).$$

If both channels are used but the opportunities of the obligation are not used, the payoff would be

$\overline{\Pi} = \frac{1}{m}(1-\alpha_P)NP_C - C_C + \frac{1}{n}\alpha'_P NP_P - \theta + \tau_E\left(\frac{1}{m}(1-\alpha_P) + \frac{1}{n}\alpha'_P\right)$. The costs for establishing the web shop and joining the platform are the same for the median seller. But due to not using the platform, the number of sales in the independent web shop is lower because the consumers leaving the platform are not directed to the channel. In fact, they are targeted by competitors. Due to these lower sales, less data is available for analysis. Accordingly, using the obligation, if data can be used, is even more attractive because more data can be generated. Therefore, the result of lemma 1, that $k = n$, also holds with data included.

(2) The second result of interest is the question of whether business users with an independent web shop are more likely to join the platform if more data can be collected for analysis. In the baseline model with data, the payoff of only using the independent web

shop is $\Pi_C = \frac{1}{m}(1-\alpha_P)NP_C - C_C + \tau_E\left(\frac{1}{m}(1-\alpha_P)\right)$. Due to joining the platform at a cost of θ, additional sales of $\frac{1}{n}\alpha_P NP_P$ can be generated. Furthermore, the new customers that are served on the platform make more data available. The difference in profit is given by $\Pi_{Diff1} = \frac{1}{n}\alpha_P NP_P - \theta + \left(\tau_E\left(\frac{1}{m}(1-\alpha_P) + \frac{1}{n}\alpha_P\right) - \tau_E\left(\frac{1}{m}(1-\alpha_P)\right)\right)$. The difference in payoff with the new obligation is denoted by:

$$\Pi_{Diff2} = \left(\frac{1}{n}\alpha_{PS}\right)NP_C + \frac{1}{n}\alpha'_P NP_P - \theta$$
$$+\left(\tau_E\left(\frac{1}{m}(1-\alpha_P) + \frac{1}{n}\alpha_{PS} + \frac{1}{n}\alpha'_P\right) - \tau_E\left(\frac{1}{m}(1-\alpha_P)\right)\right).$$

n is held constant for the moment to analyze the direct effect on the business user. Whether, in a second step, the number of business users increases or not is addressed later. The difference $\Pi_{Diff2} - \Pi_{Diff1}$ decides whether it became more attractive to join the platform or not. Aside from the benefits of data this is the same problem as in the model without data which resulted in Proposition 2. Due to higher sales, and considering the benefits of data, the additional profit from joining the platform is higher with the new obligation. The result is that the number of business users on the platform is likely to increase. Since the incentives are even higher with data, the participation is also supposed to be higher than in the model with the new obligation but without data.

As mentioned above, however, the number of business users only increases if not all businesses have already joined the platform or the costs for joining the platform are prohibitive. This result also holds if the number of business users on the platform increases, which results in more competition and, therefore, lower sales. For the first new business user, however, this effect is rather low, especially if the number of business users is high.

(3) Even without considering the benefits of data, establishing an independent web shop becomes more attractive after the introduction of the new obligation, ceteris paribus. The rationale is that additional customers can be attracted due to the obligation. Even without the obligation, the attractiveness rises because some customers directly use the web shop, and their data can be used. After the obligation, even more customers are attracted and, hence, more data can be used. Accordingly, if all business users do not already have an independent web shop or if the costs for establishing the web shop are prohibitively high, the new obligation makes web shops for business users more likely to be established. Nevertheless, an increased off-platform competition due to more web shops can limit the incentives. On the one hand, sales increase by the web shop because

new users and some old users from the platform can be served. On the other hand, data leverages this effect because additional benefits result from these additional sales. Hence, the additional data being available is supposed to increase the incentives to open an independent web shop. This result is independent of the specific player at hand.

152. Regarding data, it seems unchallenged that the data collected with the independent web shops is most valuable. Indeed, business users can analyze which products the consumer looked at before, for how long and how often and for what purchases the consumer uses the web shop. Furthermore, the business user can change the display and the functionalities, payment methods or even prices to analyze the resulting changes in consumer behavior. However, if business users rely upon the services of the platform, they have access to less granular data: the time of the purchase and the strict necessary personal data to ensure the functioning of the service or delivery of the product. With the new obligation, however, business users can have access to more valuable data from the platform. Therefore, they can adapt their strategy to effectively target users. They can analyze changes in the way they target the users on the platform and use the most effective form.

153. Although the difference in quality and amount of data is not modelled here, some results can be deduced. First, an independent web shop becomes more interesting because more valuable data can be collected than by only using the platform. Second, the new obligation makes joining the platform attractive because more data is also available by diverting some platform consumers.

2.5.4 Platform's decisions

154. With regards to the decisions by the platform, it must be mentioned that the new obligation will increase the attractiveness of becoming vertically integrated. To regain some of the consumers that are targeted by the business users, selling the goods at a net margin comparable to NP_C is attractive to the platform. To show the increased attractiveness of becoming vertically integrated, the profit of the platform must be considered. For the analysis, it is assumed, for the moment, that there is no additional cost for the platform to sell products on the platform. The platform is already established, and the standards are set by the platform itself. For a platform that is not vertically integrated, the sales before the obligation are given by $\Pi_{Platform} = \alpha_P pC_P$, that is the fee for the sales of the business users on the platform. The payoff before the obligation for a vertically integrated platform is given by $\Pi^V_{Platform} = \frac{1}{\overline{n}+1}\alpha_P NP_C + \frac{\overline{n}}{\overline{n}+1}\alpha_P pC_P$, where $\overline{n}$ denotes the number of business users on the platform before the platform becomes vertically integrated. The first term represents the sales of the platform and the second term the fees the platform receives. Note

that due to the platform stepping in, the number of competitors increases, and it is assumed that the platform users that only want to directly buy from the platform are included in α_P. The platform will become vertically integrated if $\Pi^V_{Platform} > \Pi_{Platform}$. I.e.,

$$\frac{1}{\bar{n}+1}\alpha_P NP_C + \frac{\bar{n}}{\bar{n}+1}\alpha_P pC_P > \alpha_P pC_P.$$

This holds if $NP_C > pC_P$. Considering that $NP_C = NP_P + pC_P$, becoming vertically integrated is preferred by the platform if $NP_P > 0$. A positive margin of an arbitrary business user on the platform means that margins in the independent web shops are strictly positive. Although the platform is losing some fee payments after it becomes vertically integrated, the additional sales at a high margin overcompensate the platform and, hence, vertical integration is a good choice.

After the introduction of the obligation, the number of business users increases to n' and the share α_{SP} of the demand is targeted by the business users. Accordingly, the payoff for the platform if it is not vertically integrated falls to $\Pi_{Platform} = \alpha'_P\, pC_P$, while the payoff for a vertically integrated platform is given by $\Pi^V_{Platform} = \frac{n'}{n'+1}\alpha'_P\, pC_P + \frac{1}{n'+1}\alpha'_P\, NP_C + \frac{1}{n'+1}\alpha_{PS} NP_C$. The first term represents the decreased fee payments and the second term the net profit from the sales on the platform. The third term is the profit the platform earns with consumers that are willing to leave the platform for purchases, but that were successfully targeted by the shop of the platform. Becoming vertically integrated is appealing for the platform if $\Pi^V_{Platform} > \Pi_{Platform}$. This results in the requirement that $\frac{1}{n'+1}\alpha_P NP_C > \frac{1}{n'+1}\alpha'_P\, pC_P$, because $\alpha_P = \alpha'_P + \alpha_{PS}$. Accordingly, becoming vertically integrated is more attractive if $\alpha_P NP_C > \alpha'_P\, pC_P$, which is indeed the case. The reason is that the fee payments are reduced due to the obligation in any case. This is shown by weighing the fee payments with α'_P on the right-hand side. I.e., the consumers leaving due to the obligation result in a lower potential loss in fee payments if the platform becomes vertically integrated. When a platform becomes vertically integrated and targets at least some consumers, the sales to consumers by the platform are as high as for a vertically integrated platform before the obligation. The platform acts as a competitor on the platform and targets the consumers on the platform. Furthermore, the platform can also regain some consumers that are leaving. Hence, the obligation can lead to the platform becoming active as a seller on the platform. This, however, is only the case if the platform is not active anyways. Considering the costs for becoming vertically integrated does not change the attractiveness of this change in the business model because these costs must be invested before and after the introduction of the obligation to become vertically integrated and the sales of the platform do not change.

Therefore, variable costs cannot change the results. Considering the benefits of data also does not change the findings because the amount of data available only slightly changes due to becoming vertically integrated. The platform already has the data of the consumers that are willing to leave for purchases because they have an account with the platform, for example. While being vertically integrated, the platform becomes an additional competitor on the market, which can result in lower attractiveness to business users. Nevertheless, the platform will likely gain more data for analysis compared to the situation without the obligation because joining the platform is more attractive.

Based on the assumptions so far, the entire profit of the vertically integrated platform with data and the new obligation is given by

$$\Pi^{E}_{Plattform} = \frac{\tilde{n}-1}{\tilde{n}}\alpha'_P pC_p + \frac{1}{\tilde{n}}\alpha'_P NP_C + \frac{1}{\tilde{n}}\alpha_{PS} NP_C + \tau(\alpha_P;\tilde{n}-1) - Cost\left(\frac{\tilde{n}-1}{\tilde{n}}\alpha'_P;\tilde{n}-1\right),$$

where $\tilde{n}$ denotes the total number of competitors in equilibrium on the platform, i.e., the business users and the vertically integrated platform. As mentioned in Section 2, digital platforms exhibit economies of scale. The initial costs for establishing and maintaining the platform are very high, and the variable costs for facilitating transactions are low or even zero. The *Cost* in the function, therefore, comprises high fixed costs but to some extent also variable costs based on the number of transactions and the number of business users. This is included into the model by assuming that the cost of the platform is dependent on the number of business users $\tilde{n}-1$ and the number of units sold $\frac{\tilde{n}-1}{\tilde{n}}\alpha'_P$, since the costs for the sales of the platform are included in the gross margin NP_C.

When the decision by the platform on the fee is considered, two cases must be analyzed. Under the first scenario all business users were already on the platform before the introduction of the obligation. The second case deals with a situation where not all potential business users were using the platform before the introduction of the obligation.

155. Case 1: All business users already on the platform

In the first case, the introduction of the obligation increases the attractiveness of the platform because some of the customers can be diverted from the platform to the independent web shop, which is likely to be established after the introduction, due to the higher margin. Since the platform suffers from the obligation (reduced fees), on the one hand, it eventually becomes vertically integrated, but, on the other hand, it also has an incentive to increase the fee. Before the introduction of the obligation, the business users joined the platform if $\frac{1}{\tilde{n}-1}\alpha_P NP_P + \tau_E\left(\frac{1}{\tilde{n}-1}\alpha_P + \frac{1}{m}(1-\alpha_P)\right) \geq \theta$. Note that this implies that the platform is not yet vertically integrated and the conditions for establishing an independent web shop are fulfilled. The rationale behind these assumptions is to analyze the incentives at best for the business users because the platform has not yet stepped in as a competitor. Since the business users are already on the platform, this condition for joining the platform is fulfilled.

After the introduction of the obligation and the platform becoming vertically integrated, it can be deduced that when all business users have already joined before the obligation was introduced, the attractiveness of staying on the platform even increases with the obligation. This, however, allows for an increase in the fee by the platform. The business users accept this increase because only some share of demand is affected, while an additional share is served at a higher gross margin in the web shop after the obligation. Selling on the platform even with an increased fee is also attractive because it allows for the collection of useful data. The platform, however, already has access to most of the valuable data even before the obligation because all relevant business users are on the platform. Increasing the fee, therefore, is a way to monetize the increased attractiveness.

156. Case 2: Not all business users were using the platform before the obligation

To analyze the incentives for the platform when it decides on the fees, it is assumed that the platform is vertically integrated and that the number of sellers on the platform is given by n. Furthermore, it is assumed that n is directly dependent on the amount of the fee C_P, i.e., $n(C_P)$ with $\frac{dn}{dC_P} < 0$. That means that the higher the fee charged by the platform is, the less attractive the platform is for business users and, hence, the smaller the number of business users selling via the platform. Accordingly, the profit of the platform can be rewritten as follows:

$$\Pi^{E}_{Plattform} = \alpha'_P pC_p - \frac{1}{n(C_P)}\alpha'_P pC_p + \frac{1}{n(C_P)}\alpha_P NP_C + \tau(\alpha_P; n(C_P) - 1) -$$

$Cost\left(\alpha'_P - \frac{1}{n(C_P)}\alpha'_P; n(C_P) - 1\right)$. An analysis of the first derivative to C_P reveals whether the fee rises or falls depending on the specific situation at hand. If collecting data is important for the platform and the business users are sensitive regarding their fee payments, the platform might even decrease the fee. In another case, the platform might increase the fee if it already has all the valuable information and selling directly to the consumers is attractive or business users are unlikely to leave the platform.

The effect of the obligation is also inconclusive. The first effect is that the obligation makes joining the platform more attractive. Accordingly, the platform has an incentive to increase the fee. Increasing the fee is also attractive for the platform since competition on the platform becomes more severe due to the obligation. The second effect is that the obligation reduces sales on the platform and, hence, the positive effect of an increase in the fees is lowered. Also, an increase in the fee lowers the amount of data available. The effect also depends on the business model of the platform, i.e., whether the platform was vertically integrated before the introduction of the obligation or not.

2.5.5 Summary of results

157. In essence, the obligation leads to the following potential effects even if the total amount of consumers in e-commerce is assumed to be constant:
   (a) Using the platform becomes more attractive to business users.
   (b) The obligation is also attractive and, therefore, relied upon by business users. In order to do so, they might even open up an independent web shop.
   (c) The platform has an incentive to become vertically integrated.
   (d) The amount of data available for business users and the platform is likely to increase.
   (e) Following the introduction of the obligation, the fees are likely to increase if all business users were already using the platform before. Otherwise, the effect of the obligation on the amount of the fee is indeterminate and depends on the specific manifestation of the variables.

158. The effect of a potential increase in usage of e-commerce by platforms and business users following the introduction of the obligation is left for future research. Nevertheless, if more consumers are attracted due to more sellers on the platform and more web shops in general, the effects mentioned above are likely to be reinforced.

2.6 Discussion and policy recommendations

159. First, using the platform becomes more attractive to business users. An isolated reading of this result might be alarming as the increased attractiveness of the platform could reinforce its market power. But the aim of the DMA is not to "break" big tech platforms,[9] but to lay down "rules ensuring, for all businesses, competitive and fair markets in the digital sector across the Union where gatekeepers are present, to the benefit of business users and end users" (Article 1). The Regulation also aims to

9 Proposal by Lina Khan for US Antitrust, Khan, Lina, 2019, The separation of platforms and commerce, *Columbia Law Review* 119.4

"complement the enforcement of competition law" (Recital 10), which does not sanction dominance but only its abuse (Article 102 TFEU). Nevertheless, the obligation may enhance the platform's ability to preserve its gatekeeper position and potentially increase its attractiveness, as expanded data availability could support further business growth.

160. Second, the obligation is also attractive and, therefore, used by business users. To do so, they might even open an independent web shop. This result seems to lead to more competition on the downstream market, which is beneficial for consumers. The platform, facing downstream competition, might in the first place be incentivized to lower its commission to compete with the prices directly set in the web shops of the business users. However, a consumer receiving multiple messages from different sellers via the platform and a message directly from the platform might, due to the absence of switching costs, buy directly from the platform. This insight is based on the next result.

161. Third, the platform has an incentive to become vertically integrated. Vertical integration creates efficiencies, eliminates double marginalization, and hence can be beneficial for consumers. However, the efficiencies of vertical integration can be counterbalanced by the risks of anticompetitive practices if the platform has significant market power. The anticompetitive risks of vertical integration have been discussed in the literature from the perspective of self-preferencing practices (Demary/Engels/Rusche, 2020). Padilla et al. (2022) built a two-period model to analyze under which conditions a monopolist selling devices has the ability and incentives to abuse its dominant position via self-preferencing practices. They found that during the second period the gatekeeper is incentivized to privilege its own product instead of third-party sellers on his platform if it faces slow or negative growth of demand for the devices the platform sells. These concerns are anchored in the DMA since self-preferencing practices from a gatekeeper are banned per Art. 6 (5). Compliance with the obligations in Art. 6 may be further specified by the Commission, and the gatekeeper can request that the Commission determine whether the measures it intends to implement to ensure compliance are effective (Art. 8 (3)).

162. Fourth, the amount of data available for business users and the platform is likely to increase. The Crémer report (2019) recommends as desirable "the broadest dissemination and use of data by the greatest number of firms." However, an increase in the amount of data available for business users and for the platform may not have the same effect, depending on their capacity to collect and process the data. It is assumed that the platform, which is already collecting and processing huge amount of data, would have the necessary investments to support and benefit from this increase, while it would require additional investment for small business users. Hence, the platforms are likely to benefit more than the business users.

163. In the long term, small business users will benefit from an increase in the data available but will first have to bear costs to collect and process the data. An increase in the amount of data for the platform may result in a reinforcement of its market position in the short term. However, and since data is one of the key inputs on digital markets, the DMA also includes specific obligations to ensure a level playing field and fairness between gatekeepers and business users regarding the collection and processing of data. For example, Article 5 (2), 6 (2), 6 (9) of the DMA pursue this end. The additional cost for monetizing data that have to be borne by business users can incentivize them, especially SMEs, to use the services of the platform instead. This then leads to the negative consequences for the business users described by Kraemer, Schnurr and Wohlfarth (2019). In Germany, for example, the project Incentives and Economics of Data Sharing[10] is funded by the Federal Ministry of Education and Research in order to set the stage for the participation of companies in interorganizational data exchange. Such projects are important for helping companies in the EU to take advantage of the opportunities of the data economy. A coordination of such efforts between the member states and support for member states that do not have the means, however, is important for improving the EU in the global digital economy competition. Another field of public investment is that of the digital infrastructure in the EU. An analysis in the context of the Digital Economy and Society Index (DESI) showed a severe difference in the quality of the digital infrastructure for enterprises between member states (Eurostat, 2022).

164. Also based on data is the insight that merger control gains in importance when data is also considered. The rationale behind this is that large digital corporations with enormous amounts of data are also willing to acquire small companies with valuable data sets at matchlessly high prices (Buechel/Rusche, 2021). The DMA increases competition on the platform and off the platform. Merger control has to ensure that the platform cannot improve its position in competition by mergers and acquisitions.

165. Fifth, following the introduction of the obligation, the fees are likely to increase if all business users were already using the platform before. Otherwise, the effect of the obligation on the amount of the fee is indeterminate. Increasing demand, however, can also lead to higher fees even if not all business users use the platform. Facing higher fees, the business users have the choice to integrate the increase of the fee in their costs or to pass on the increase to their consumers. In the event of a passed-on fee, the consumers are worse off, and this is one of the concerns of the EU Commission in the case brought by Spotify against the App Store. The proportional fees are the other side of the coin in the anti-steering

10 https://ieds-projekt.de/

clauses in the on-going case law related to the digital market. However, if the DMA prohibits anti-steering clauses, there is nothing prohibiting the imposition (or increase) of fees by the gatekeeper on its business partners. The lack of provisions on the increase in fees imposed by the platform on its business users makes sense because the Regulation introduced *per-se* rules and this increase would require a effects analysis. Hence, the cases on anti-steering clauses that we presented are a perfect example of the upcoming complementary application between the DMA and competition law.

166. According to Bostoen (2023), the DMA targets App Store fees with the FRAND obligations contained in Article 6 (12) DMA. While this possibility was already raised in the JRC report by economic experts, they underlined that it was not clear whether the provision addresses price discrimination and monopolistic pricing. During the third workshop held by the Commission for the DMA, the FRAND general conditions of access for business users to software app stores were discussed. Ribera Martínez (2023) outlined the main takeaways of the workshop, and it would seem that Article 6 (12) could fall under different interpretations, both as a substantive and a procedural provision, which could work either as a mandate that the conditions of access are set out in a fair and objective procedure or that the EU Commission may be required to set the fair and reasonable standards to satisfy the requirements of the FRAND conditions. Therefore, there is not yet a definitive answer on whether the DMA – though it contains FRAND obligations – could or would leave the floor to competition law enforcement. It is also unclear whether the FRAND obligations in the DMA could target the amount of the application stores' proportional fees.

167. On the policy recommendations, if the DMA aims to ensure competitiveness and fairness on digital markets between gatekeepers and business users, to the benefit of both business users and end users, we would recommend not reducing competition law efforts. All the anticompetitive practices are not covered by the DMA, as it is not its aim, so there is still a need for competition law enforcement on platforms markets, especially for anticompetitive practices requiring a by-effect analysis. However, considering that some of the obligations of the DMA were based on legal proceedings, there are two pillars that are important for competition in the digital economy. The first pillar is to improve legal certainty and reduce complexity and the duration of the proceedings regarding the abuse of dominance in Article 102 TFEU (Schweitzer, 2023). The second pillar is the incorporation of new findings in competition law into new obligations in the DMA, which can be done using the Review process laid down in Article 53 of the DMA.

168. Will business users and end users ultimately be better off after the introduction of the DMA? The rules introduced in the DMA are to the benefit

of both business users and end users and certainly create the right sets of incentives for a more competitive and fair digital market. However, the DMA only targets gatekeepers with a limited set of obligations and regulating their relationship with business users. Therefore, end users still face a variety of legal and economic risks that are not captured by the DMA. These risks should be mapped (from information asymmetry, decrease in autonomy and innovations, dark patterns...) as well as their interplay and the efficiency of their private and public enforcement. On the side of business users, the welfare effect of the obligations might be different between small and medium-sized companies and whether they are already on the market or are planning to enter the market. In this case, small companies, which would benefit from the obligations imposed on the platform, might not have the financial capacity to make the investment for entering the market (standardization of their product to the platform's standard).

169. While the gatekeepers are not yet designated at the time of writing this paper, Grafunder et al. (2022) report what seems to be early implementation choices from some potential gatekeepers. Among them, Google announced that that it would also direct European developers to use alternative payment systems and explicitly referred to this as an early effort to comply with the DMA. With regards to Google's anti-steering clauses, despite the DMA not being applicable to the United Kingdom, the platform will have to apply changes to its rules and allow app developers to use alternative billing systems for in-app purchases. In the context of an investigation by the UK Competition and Market Authority, Google also offered commitments to reduce its service fee.[11] The upcoming designation of gatekeepers and the imposition of the obligations contained in the DMA is definitely shaking up the digital industry and is already providing incentives for fairer and more contestable market.

11 UK CMA, Proposed commitments regarding changes to Google Play's rules to allow certain app developers to use alternative billing systems for in-app purchases, April 19, 2023. Last accessed on June 1, 2023: https://www.gov.uk/government/consultations/proposed-commitments-regarding-changes-to-google-plays-rules-to-allow-certain-app-developers-to-use-alternative-billing-systems-for-in-app-purchases

2.7 Bibliography

Alexandrov, A., Deltas, G., & Spulber, D. F. "Antitrust and competition in two-sided markets."*Journal of Competition Law and Economics*, 7(4), (2011):775-812.

Auer, Soeren et al. "Industrial Data Space: Digital Souvereignity Over Data." White Paper Munich (2016).

Authority for Consumers & Markets. "Apple changes unfair conditions, allows alternative payments methods in dating apps." (2022) https://www.acm.nl/en/publications/acm-apple-changes-unfair-conditions-allows-alternative-payments-methods-dating-apps [29.8.2021]

Bostoen, Friso. "Understanding the Digital Markets Act" *The Antitrust Bulletin* 68.2 (2023): 263-306.

Buchholtz, Sonia; Bukowski, Maciej; Śniegocki, Aleksander. "Big and open data in Europe. A growth engine or a missed opportunity?" *Warsaw Institute for Economic Studies (WISE Institute)* (2014)

Buechel, Jan and Rusche, Christian. "Competition in the digital Economy. An analysis of Gatekeepers and Regulations." *IW-Policy Paper* No. 26 Cologne (2020).

Buechel, Jan and Rusche, Christian. "On Gatekeepers and Structural Competition Problems." *Intereconomics* Vol. 56 No. 4 (2021):205-210.

Buechel, Jan; Demary, Vera; Engels, Barbara; Graef, Inge; Koppel, Oliver; Rusche, Christian. "Innovationen in der Plattformökonomie. Eine ökonomische und rechtliche Analyse, Study for the German Commission of Experts for Research and Innovation (EFI)." Cologne (2022).

Buechel, Jan and Engels, Barbara. "Datenbewirtschaftung von Unternehmen in Deutschland." *IW-Trends* Vol. 49 No. 1 (2022):73-90.

Cabral, L., Haucap, J., Parker, G., Petropoulos, G., Valletti, T., and Van Alstyne, M., "The EU Digital Markets Act." *Publications Office of the European Union* ISBN 978-92-76-29788-8 doi:10.2760/139337, JRC122910 (2021).

Chaiehloudj Walid. "United States: The US Supreme Court rules that the credit card market is a multisided market and that anti-steering clauses do not have anticompetitive effects on this market (*American Express*)." *Concurrences* N° 4-2018 Art. N° 88296 (2018): 209-212.

Chaiehloudj Walid. "Will digital regulation law marginalize competition law? Reflections in the light of *Epic Games v. Apple.*" *Concurrences* N° 3-2021, Art. N° 101310 (2021).

Choi, Jay Pil. "Tying in two-sided markets with multi-homing." *CESifo Working Paper* No. 2073 Center for Economic Studies and ifo Institute (CESifo) Munich (2007).

Colangelo, Margherita. "Traditional and Platform MFN Clauses under Antitrust Law: Insights from Recent Practice." *Policy International Antitrust Chronicle* (2019).

Crémer, Jacques; de Montjoye, Yves-Alexander; Schweitzer, Heike. "Competition policy for the digital era." Final report for the European Commission (2019).

Decarolis, F., & Li, M. "Regulating online search in the EU: From the Android case to the Digital Markets Act and Digital Services Act." *International Journal of Industrial Organization*, 102983 (2023).

Demary, Vera and Rusche, Christian. "The Economics of Platforms." IW-Analyse No. 123 Cologne (2018).

Demary, Vera; Guggenberger, Nikolas; Rabovskaja, Elisaweta; Rusche, Christian. Data Sharing im E-Commerce: Rechtliche und ökonomische Grundlagen, Gutachten im Auftrag der ServiCon Service & Consult eG, Cologne (2019).

Demary, Vera; Engels, Barbara; Rusche, Christian. "Differentiated Treatment of Business Users by Online Platforms – An Analysis of Incentives with an In-Depth Look at App Stores and E-Commerce Platforms." *Observatory on the Online Platform Economy, Analytical paper* 2, Cologne (2020).

European Commission. "Impact Assessment Report, Accompanying the document: Proposal for a Regulation of the European Parliament and of the Council on contestable and fair markets in the digital sector (Digital Markets Act)." *Commission staff working document* Part 1/2, SWD(2020) 363 final, Brussels (2020).

European, Commission. "Antitrust: Commission sends Statement of Objections to Apple on App Store rules for music streaming providers." Press release https://ec.europa.eu/commission/presscorner/detail/en/ip_21_2061 [Aug. 29, 2022] (2021).

European Commission. Directorate-General for Justice and Consumers, Lupiáñez-Villanueva, F., Boluda, A., Bogliacino, F., et al., "Behavioural study on unfair commercial practices in the digital environment: dark patterns and manipulative personalisation: final report." *Publications Office of the European Union* (2022).

European Commission. "Antitrust: Commission sends Statement of Objections to Apple clarifying concerns over App Store rules for music streaming providers." Press release https://ec.europa.eu/commission/presscorner/detail/en/ip_23_1217 [May 30, 2023] (2023).

Eurostat. Type of connections to the internet [ISOC_CI_IT_EN2__custom_2840229], The speed of the fixed line connection(s) to the internet is sufficient for the actual needs of the enterprise, All enterprises, without financial sector (10 or more employees and self-employed persons), accessed on June 1, 2022.

Filistrucchi, Lapo, Damien Geradin, Eric Van Damme, and Pauline Affeldt. "Market definition in two-sided markets: Theory and practice." *Journal of Competition Law and Economics* 10, no. 2 (2014): 293-339.

Grafunder René, Stefanowicz-Barańska Agnieszka, Tamke Maren, Marek Maciej. "EU Digital Markets Act: next steps and long-term outlook.", last accessed on June 1, 2023: Dentons – EU Digital Markets Act: next steps and long-term outlook (2022)

Hotelling, Harold. "Stability in Competition." *The Economic Journal* Vol. 39 No. 153 (1929):41-57.

Khan, Lina. "The separation of platforms and commerce." *Columbia Law Review* 119.4 (2019).

Klemperer, Paul. "The Competitiveness of Markets with Switching Costs." *RAND Journal of Economics* Vol 18 No. 1, (1987):138–150.

Kraemer, Jan; Schnurr, Daniel; Wohlfarth, Michael. "Trapped in the Data-Sharing Dilemma." *MIT Sloan management review* Vol. 60 No. 2 (2019): 22-23.

Lin, Xiaogang; Zhou, Yong-Wu; Xie, Wei; Zhong, Yuanguang; Cao, Bin. "Pricing and Product-bundling Strategies for E-commerce Platforms with Competition." *European Journal of Operational Research* Vol. 283 No. 3 (2020):1026-1039.

Luo, Xiaoxiao; Li, Minqiang; Feng, Haiyang; Feng, Nan. "Intertemporal mixed bundling strategy of information products with network externality."*Computers and Industrial Engineering* Vol 113 November 2017 (2017) 369-381.

Mandrescu, Daniel. "Tying and bundling by online platforms – Distinguishing between lawful expansion strategies and anti-competitive practices." *Computer Law & Security Review* Vol. 40 105499 (2021).

McMahon, Kathryn. "USA: Monopolization of mobile ecosystems – The decision in *Epic v. Apple*." *Concurrences* N° 3-2022, Art. N° 107327 (2022).

Meijer, Rogier and Timmerman Sander. "The Rotterdam District Court largely denies a Big Tech company's requests to block the Dutch Competition Authority's publication of decision and fines in abuse of dominance case against dating-app developers *(Apple)." e-Competitions* December 2021 Art. N° 105395 (2021).

Moody, Daniel and Walsh, Peter. "Measuring The Value Of Information. An Asset Valuation Approach" Paper presented at the Seventh European Conference on Information Systems (ECIS'99) (1999).

Official Journal of the European Union. Regulation (EU) 2022/1925 of the European Parliament and of the Council of 14 September 2022 on contestable and fair markets in the digital sector and amending Directives (EU) 2019/1937 and (EU) 2020/1828 (Digital Markets Act), L 265, Vol. 65, (2022):1-6665.

Padilla, Jorge; Perkins, Joe; Piccolo, Salvatore. "Self-Preferencing in Markets with Vertically Integrated Gatekeeper Platforms." *The Journal of Industrial Economics* 70 371(2022).

Petit, Nicolas. "The proposed digital markets act (DMA): A legal and policy review." *Journal of European Competition Law & Practice* 12.7: (2021):529-541.

Pino, Flavio. "The microeconomics of data – a survey." *Journal of Industrial and Business* Economics 49 (2022): 635-665.

Prasad, Ashutosh; Venkatesh, R.; Mahajan, Vijay. "Optimal Bundling of Technological Products with Network Externality." *Management Science* Vol. 56 No. 12 (2010):2224-2236.

Reuters. "Epic Games asks US Supreme Court let App Store order take effect." https://www.reuters.com/legal/epic-games-asks-us-supreme-court-let-app-store-order-take-effect-2023-07-27/ [Sept. 14, 2023] (2023).

Ribera Martínez, Alba. "Third Workshop on the DMA – This is not a Blueprint for the DMA: The Proof of the App-Store Pudding is in the eating." *Kluwer Competition Law Blog* (2023).

Rochet, Jean Charles and Tirole, Jean. "Tying in two-sided markets and the honor all cards rule." *International Journal of Industrial Organization* Vol. 26 No. 6 (2008):1333-1347.

Schweitzer, Heike. "Art. 102 AEUV: Irrwege und Auswege, in: Wirtschaft und Wettbewerb." Vol. 73 No. 2 (2023): 61.

Shapiro, Carl and Varian, Hal R. "Information Rules. A Strategic Guide to the Network Economy." *Harvard Business Press* (1999).

Sun, Keke. "Bundling, Vertical Differentiation, and Platform Competition." *Review of Network Economics* Vol. 17,no. 1 (2018):1-23.

Sun, Jing; Fu, Xin; Cai, Shun; Shi, Hai-Rong. "Dynamic Optimal Pricing Strategies for Knowledge-Sharing Platforms". PACIS 2018 Proceedings, 272, https://aisel.aisnet.org/pacis2018/272 (2018).

Spulber, D. F. *Market Microstructure: Intermediaries and the Theory of the Firm.* New York: Cambridge University Press. (1999)

Supreme Court of the United States, 2023, Case Number (21-16695), https://www.supremecourt.gov/search.aspx?filename=/docket/docketfiles/html/public/23a78.html [Sept. 14, 2023]

Whinston, Michael D. "Tying, Foreclosure, and Exclusion." *The American Economic Review* Vol. 80 No. 4 (1990):837–859

Chapter 3
Auditing the ranking strategy of a marketplace's algorithm in the frame of competition law commitments with surrogate models: the Amazon's Buy Box case

Essay co-autored with Benoit Rottembourg, Inria, Regalia.[1] *In a global context where competition authorities are investigating and sanctioning Amazon's marketplace for practices of self-preferencing at the expense of their business users and consumers (Italian AGCM 2021, EU Commission 2022, UK CMA 2024, US FTC on-going since 2023), we observe a trend of imposing remedies on dominant players in digital markets. In addition, the Digital Markets Act, shifting from an ex-post enforcement approach to ex-ante obligations on designated gatekeepers, is strengthening auditing power over these gatekeepers, which risk heavier penalties in the event of non-compliance. Therefore, competition authorities and regulators need tools to audit the compliance of these dominant players in the e-commerce sector over the obligations and remedies they are imposing on dynamic, and personalized algorithms. Most of these algorithms embed Machine-Learning components, introducing opacity and potentially biases in the decision-making process. The aim of the paper is to explore the benefits of using black-box auditing techniques to provide insights into the behavior of these online algorithms. We anchor our research in the literature of product prominence from vertically integrated players, of choice ranking, and of the specific literature related to Amazon search ranking, automatic pricing and Buy Box's algorithms. Through a study of the pricing and ranking of several thousand*

1 The information and views set out in this article are those of the author and do not necessarily reflect the official opinion of the European Commission.

products on Amazon, from 2017 to 2023, we illustrate the potential of surrogate models. While our dataset only covers some categories on Amazon.fr, the large number of competitions allowed us to demonstrate, with a 94% accuracy, that the variable isAmazon, or variables correlated to it, had a positive effect on winning Buy Box before mid-2022, and that this positive effect has decreased after mid-2022. In our research, the machine learnings models revealed a significantly higher degree of accuracy and sensitivity compared to a logistic regression, opening the discussion on the added value and role of surrogate models based on machine learning techniques in guiding the auditor, as well as raising the question of their probative value in the regulatory context.

3.1 Introduction

170. This paper proposes a methodology to conduct an *ex post* audit, within the regulatory framework, of concerns related to self-preferencing in a marketplace's ranking algorithm. We rely on the European Union (EU) Commission decision in December 2022, imposing remedies on Amazon's Buy Box, as a case study.

171. Amazon is a vertically integrated online marketplace platform on which third-party sellers meet buyers, and on which Amazon also markets its own-brand products. In addition, the platform has developed complementary offerings for third-party sellers (in terms of logistics, commercial data, and cloud services) as well as for consumers (a fast delivery service, video and audio streaming, etc.). There are several algorithms at work on Amazon marketplace, among which, a search engine algorithm (Subhradeep et al., 2022), a pricing algorithm (Fry and Manna, 2016), an algorithm to treat reviews (Seele et al., 2021). In this paper we focus on the Amazon Buy Box algorithm, meaning, the algorithm that determines the seller who wins the Buy Box for a determined product, when there are several sellers. The Buy Box is a privileged ranking position on the product detail page and which only displays the top recommended offer.

172. The EU Commission opened a formal investigation in November 2020 under the concerns over a bias in granting sellers' access to its Buy Box, leading to a preferential treatment of Amazon's own retail business and sellers using Amazon's logistics and delivery services. Amazon submitted a first set of commitments on the 8th of July 2022[2], to address the Buy Box concern, which included: treating all sellers equally when ranking the offers for the purposes of the selection of the Buy Box winner, displaying a second competing offer to the Buy Box winner

2 Press release, Commission seeks feedback on commitments offered by Amazon concerning marketplace seller data and access to Buy Box and Prime, 14 July 2019, available at: https://ec.europa.eu/commission/presscorner/detail/en/ip_22_4522

if there is a second offer from a different seller that is sufficiently differentiated from the first one on price and/or delivery. This first set of commitments were subject to a Commission's market test, in which all interested third parties were consulted to verify whether these commitments would remove all the competition concerns. Following the results of the market test,[3] Amazon amended its initial proposal on the 22nd of November 2022. On the 20th of December 2022, the EU Commission accepted commitments from Amazon to treat equally all sellers when ranking the offers for the purposes of the selection of the Buy Box winner.[4]

173. This case study triggered our attention in a global context of an increase of commitment decisions following concerns of abuse of dominance in digital markets.[5] The Amazon's Buy Box is prone to generate a distortion of competition for complementors while exploiting the constrained rationality of the consumers. This potential distortion of competition occurs with the vertically integrated platform preferencing its own services. In this particular case study, the self-preferencing operates through discriminating conditions in the ranking algorithm. Auditing a recommendation algorithm *per se* already raises challenges (Metaxa et al., 2021; Mullainathan et al., 2012; Gaddis, 2018), but in this case study, the remedies aim to restore the competitive process, adding an extra challenge. Once the regulator identifies the concerns and accept the commitments by the undertaking, the trustee is in charge of monitoring the implementation of the commitment decision. It is in this very technical context, of imposing remedies on a ranking algorithm requiring ex-post monitoring, that we are comparing the pros and cons of potential methodological framework through surrogate models.

174. We propose a methodology framework to audit a ranking algorithm of a digital market, demonstrating the contribution of surrogate models. In this paper, we collect data from an API price tracker and then compare a logistic regression with modern machine learning methods to demonstrate the added value of using more sophisticated technologies. We claim that the latter provide sensitivity analysis offering richer insight to the auditor. Finally, we try to identify whether there is an evolution of the key

---

3 The market test can be framed as a game of revelation of information and lobbying in which the competitors and third parties have the incentive to ask for better commitments from the firm under scrutiny, and the Commission aims to find an equilibrium between the firm's proposal and competitors' concerns.

4 Press release, Commission accepts commitments by Amazon barring it from using marketplace seller data, and ensuring equal access to Buy Box and Prime, 20 December 2022, available at: https://ec.europa.eu/commission/presscorner/detail/en/ip_22_7777

5 The OECD issues a report in 2022 on remedies and commitments in abuse cases and found around 30% of abuse of dominance cases with settlement or commitments in OECD countries in 2020, and around 40% for Europe countries16. The issuance of the report was fuelled, among other reasons, by the growing number of enforcement actions against digital platforms. Digital markets characteristics can be specifically challenging when it comes to designing remedies. Indeed, the digital sector is deemed to be fast-moving and intensely innovative which can render remedies ineffective if market conditions quickly alter over time.

explanatory variables over time and whether we can identify a tipping point. In terms of expected results, a tipping point in our models would be a differentiation event in the platform's algorithm, which, in our case analysis, could be interpreted as an attempt to comply with the remedies imposed by the regulator.

175. We anchor our research in the literature of product prominence from vertically integrated players (Cure et al., 2022), of choice ranking (Grobvic and Chen, 2018), and of the specific literature related to Amazon search ranking, automatic pricing and Buy Box's algorithms (Chen et al., 2016; Gómez-Losada et al., 2022; Hunold et al., 2022; Farronato et al., 2023; Raval 2023; Waldfogel, 2024; Dash et al., 2024).

176. First, we review the literature. Then, we present our research method, from the data collection to the three steps research method applied. Finally, we discuss our results and provide policy recommendations for remedies imposed on ranking algorithms in digital markets.

3.2 Review of literature

177. There are several trade-offs between using a commitment decision versus sanctioning an infringement in EU competition law competition law. Both the EU Commission and the companies investigated benefit from procedural economy gains of settlement: it is cheaper and faster to settle rather than litigate, settlements are pragmatic (Dunne, 2014). However, commitments decisions results in costs: loss of enforcement of Article 102 (in terms of clarification of the law, public censure, deterrence, punishment, disgorgement of illicit gains) (Wils, 2008) and cost of supervision of the commitments. Settling comes at the cost of learning from enforcement of competition law (Steviev, 2014).

178. Choné et al. (2014) and Gautier and Petit (2018) discuss the optimality of commitments decisions and its interaction with formal infringement decisions in EU competition law. Feasey & Krämer (2019) study how to remedy "intermediation biases" by vertically integrated companies. Hoehn (2020) discusses the challenges of designing and implementing behavioural remedies in the digital economy. Petit and Gal (2021) consider three radical restorative remedies for digital markets: mandatory sharing of algorithmic learning, subsidisation of competitors and temporary shutdown.

179. With specific regards to Amazon's algorithm, Janger & Twerski (2019) challenge the myth that Amazon is a neutral intermediation platform between sellers and buyers. On the contrary, Amazon has implemented several strategies, including the Buy Box, enabling it to control each sale and maximise its profits. Yet, these mechanisms are not transparent to the consumer nor to the seller. This deconstruction of the platform's

neutrality is also illustrated by its pricing algorithm. Chen et al (2016) gathered four months of data on all merchants on the Amazon platform selling one of the 1,641 top-selling products of their sample with the aim of detecting automated pricing algorithm strategies. The results of their study does not show a clear advantage for cases where Amazon is a seller but demonstrated that sellers who might use pricing algorithms are more frequently winners of the Buy Box, which would have the effect of exacerbating a disparity between algorithmic sellers and non-algorithmic third-party sellers.

180. Specific to self-preferencing practices, Farronato et al. (2023) study whether Amazon is engaging in self-preferencing practices in search ranking products looking at real consumer search data. The sample studied by the authors covered 3,019 unique searches by 184 users. Looking at the data on search users, it confirms that ranking matters since 72,1 percent of search users did not click past the first page. The authors found that Amazon brand was a meaningful predictor in search results, suggesting self-preferencing practices from the platform. Dash et al., 2024 further researched a series of empirical investigations as to whether Amazon engages in self-preferencing in relation to Amazon's Buy Box, offer listings pages, Alexa Search and recommendation systems.

181. Specific to the Amazon's Buy Box, Etumnu (2022) studies the performance of third-party sellers against Amazon by distinguishing between products that are sold and shipped by Amazon, those sold by the third-party seller and shipped by Amazon and those sold and shipped by a third-party merchant. Etumnu observes equivalent performance between the first two categories, depending on whether the product is sold by Amazon or by a third-party seller using Amazon's logistics, and weak performance for the last category, but cannot draw any conclusions about the implementation of anti-competitive practices. Gómez-Losada et al. (2022) studied twenty-two products on the Amazon page in Italy over a period of ten months and carried out two experiments with the aim of estimating the characteristics considered by Amazon in order for a seller to appear in the purchase box. One of the experiments involved predicting which seller would appear in the Buy Box. The authors noted that the consumer's experience and the price dynamics of the sellers were criteria taken into account when ranking the Buy Box. Raval (2023) studies Amazon's algorithm rules to determine which seller wins the Buy Box and to measure Amazon's self-preferencing practices. The interpretation of his results shows self-preferencing practices in favor of Amazon's retail and Amazon fulfilment. There is also a preference for Amazon Retail over third party FBA offers. Waldfogel (2024) empirically studies Amazon's own search ranks on the marketplace in the context of the entry of the DMA which prohibits self-preferencing. The author finds that shortly after the EU Commission designated Amazon

as a "gatekeeper", the Amazon rank differential fell from a 30 position advantage to a 20 position advantage, compared to other major brands' rank positions which were unaffected.

182. Summarizing from an economics risk assessment perspective[6]: Amazon is a vertically integrated platform, with the resources to implement self-preferencing practices. If the product presented in the Buy Box is the result of a biased ranking, and not the best product (according to determined criteria), there is manipulation of the information provided to the consumers and a diversion of demand from potential winning sellers. Furthermore, the Buy Box has been qualified as "unavoidable" for consumers, they are nudged to select the seller winning the Buy Box over any other sellers.

3.3 Method

3.3.1 Framework of the research methodology

183. The closest paper to our research in terms of method is the paper from Raval (2023) that aims to study Amazon's algorithm rules to determine which seller wins the Buy Box and to measure Amazon's self-preferencing practices. Raval collected data from several countries (US, UK, Germany, France) and product categories between December 9, 2020 and January 29, 2021. To predict which offer wins the Buy Box, the author estimates a multinomial logit model. The empirical model from Raval is an example of an explanatory linear regression. In this essay, differentiating from the model from Raval, we use data collected on Amazon.fr only, we collected less products and sellers' data but more granular data. Raval compared the approximations of his empirical model with the actual winners of the Buy Box, and his model correctly predicted the Buy Box offer 88% of the time across all categories and 80% of the time for products with multiple offers.

184. We use the same source of data collection as Raval. However, we restrict both geographic scope to our data set, only focusing on France, and we collect data from less categories, with the aim to have for each ASIN[7] at least three sellers on average over the last 90 days prior to the data collection. Hence, we restricted the scope but with the aim to achieve higher granularity. Keepa maintains price histories for all products on Amazon, and allows searches by categories of products, ASIN or seller identification.

185. We aim to test the following hypotheses. First, we complement a logistical regression with more sophisticated machine learning methods, relying on

6 For a survey on the economics literature of hybrid marketplaces with a focus on Amazon and self-preferencing, see Etro (2023).

7 An ASIN is the Amazon Standard Identification Number, to identify a product.

the hypothesis that machine learning methods will improve the accuracy of our model and capture more sensitivity to variable changes. Second, we make the hypothesis that before the implementation of the remedies our model will show the importance of the variable *isAmazon* as reflecting self-preferencing practices. This finding will be aligned with the literature (Raval, 2023). Third, we expect the importance of the variable *isAmazon* to decrease in the course of the negotiation and pre-implementation of the remedies, which could either indicate a decrease or a cease of self-preferencing from Amazon.

186. We built and compared four models in order to identify the influence of variables in the Buy Box winning decision. The logit regression and the decision tree optimize for a set of parameters, with either a set of coefficients or one tree. The random forest and gradient boosting methods are ensemble methods, hence iterative approaches. In the random forest method, 10% of the data or a column are removed from the first tree, and this is repeated 100 or 150 times. In the gradient boosting method, the second tree learns from the "mistakes" of the first tree and this is repeated 100 or 150 times. All four models use the same characteristics to describe an offer by a seller for a given product:

- Year and Month of the BuyBox competition
- Price of the offer
- isPrime (when the offer is compatible with the prime program of Amazon): True/False
- isMAP[8]: True/False
- isShippable[9]: True/False
- isAddonItem[10]: True/False
- isPreorder: True/False
- isWarehouseDeal[11]: True/False
- isScam[12]: True/False
- isPrimeExcl (exclusive for Prime customers): True/False
- isFBA[13]: True/False

8 From Keepa API description: is MAP means "if the price of this offer is hidden on Amazon due to a MAP (minimum advertised price) restriction.

9 From Keepa API description: False to is Shippable might mean that the offer is temporarily out of stock or a pre-order.

10 From Amazon's website: "Add-on items" https://www.amazon.com/gp/help/customer/display.html/ref=hp_468520_buyaddon?nodeId=200876660

11 From Amazon's website: "Warehouse deals" for second-hand products https://www.amazon.fr/Offres-Reconditionnees-Toutes-Les-Offres/b?ie=UTF8&node=8873224031

12 From Keepa API description: is Scam is a "Boolean value indicating whether or not our system identified that the offering merchants attempts to scam users".

13 Frm Keppa API description: is FBA "whether or not this offer is fulfilled by Amazon".

- shipsFromChina: True/False
- allTimePositiveRating: 0-100, in percent
- allTimeRatingCount: number of ratings

187. Our approach consists in building every pair of offers, o1 and o2 (we have close to one million such pairs in our dataset) that compete for the Buy Box for a given product, when at least one of them wins the Buy Box, and try to predict which offer is the most likely to win the Box. For each characteristic of the offers we compute the difference between o1 and o2 and the model "learns" the effect of this set of differences on the result when o1 beats o2 (and win the Buy Box) or the converse.

188. As shown above, the variables at stake are mainly categorical and even binary variables (with values taken in the set {True, False}). Their difference for a couple of offers is still categorical. Only the price, the positive rating percentage and the rating count can be considered as continuous variables, so is their difference. As frequently mentioned in the literature of e-commerce classification algorithms, tree-based methods are known to out-perform both linear models and neural network techniques when large tabular (and often categorical) data is concerned. For a survey on application of Machine Learning techniques in e-commerce we refer to (Mice et al., 2019; Policarpo et al., 2021; Bertolini et al., 2021).

189. Within the family of Machine Learning techniques, tree ensemble methods and boosting techniques – like Random Forests or Gradient Boosting models –, have performance and robustness properties that make them the solution of choice in e-commerce classification and ranking solutions (Breiman, 1996 & 2001; Friedman, 2001; Chen and Guestrin, 2016; Prokhorenkova et al., 2018). More recently, a comparison between tree ensemble methods and neural networks (or deep learning techniques) for tabular data classification problems can be found in Shwartz-Ziv and Armon (2022) and Grinsztajn et al. (2022). They assess the performance of tree ensemble methods.

190. It is likely that Amazon itself relies on such techniques to produce its ranking and elect the Buy Box winner, the one that maximizes the economic value for the platform. Thus, we have developed and trained four classic classification models, two explainable ones – a multinomial regression and a decision tree (Breiman et al. 1984) – and two machine learning models, a Random Forest (Breiman, 2001) and a Gradient Boosting (Chen and Guestrin, 2016). In the following we will name those models respectively: "logit", "decision_tree", "random_forest", and "gradient_boosting". We deliberately limited ourselves to the basic characteristics of the offers and did not add external variables or knowledge. Similarly, we did not optimize the parameters of the four models intensively to compare them in a fair manner.

3.3.2 Data collection

191. The data was collected from Keepa, a third-party API for Amazon, tracking all products available in US, Germany, UK, France, Italy, Spain, Canada, Japan, India, Mexico, and Brazil. Each product is identified by an Amazon Single Identification Number (ASIN).

192. However, we restrict both geographic scope to our data set, only focusing on France, and we collect data from less categories, with the aim to have for each ASIN at least three sellers on average over the last 90 days prior to the data collection.

193. We decided to arbitrarily focus on the top 7 categories of Raval's sample in number of offers (median and average): books, CDs, DVDs, videogames, toys, tools, and sport.

194. We collected the ASINs on these seven categories whenever the new offer count was greater than 3 on average on the last 90 days. We also collected ASINs on several sub-categories of these six categories with the same rule of collecting ASIN whenever the new offer count was greater than 3 on average on the last 90 days. The table below summarizes all the categories of products on which ASIN data was collected as well as the number of ASINs:

Category	**Sub-category**	**90dav.: New offers count greater than 3 (number of ASINs)**
Books		50
Books	Bandes dessinées	54
Books	Roman et littérature	17
Books	Tourisme et voyage	80
CDs		81
CDs	Musique classique	91
CDs	Pop	88
CDs	Jazz	84
DVDs & Blu-ray		54
DVDs & Blu-ray	Films	58
DVDs & Blu-ray	Séries TV	76
DVDs & Blu-ray	Actions et aventures	63
Videogames		64
Videogames	Xbox ones: jeux consoles accessoires	51
Videogames	Jeux vidéos PC: jeux et accessoires	57
Toys		72
Toys	Jeux de société	77
Toys	Jouets radiocommandés	24
Toys	Maquette et modélisme	72

Category	Sub-category	90dav.: New offers count greater than 3 (number of ASINs)
Tools		36
Tools	Quincaillerie	38
Sport		30
Sport	Cyclisme	28
Sport	Vêtements de sport	32
Sport	Sports nautiques	84

195. The dataset created has 91,000 offers for 9,486 sellers. For 11% of the offers Amazon is the seller. The oldest offer is from the 22/06/2016 and the most recent on the 06/09/2023. On the dataset we found around 80,000 observations in which with have a unique Buy Box's winning offer. Therefore, we could create about 1,6 million competitions between the winning offer and every non-winning offer. Unfortunately, due to the lack of access to rankings, for offers not winning the Buy Box, we had to limit our competitions to competitions with the winner. When competitions had no winners at all, we eliminated the corresponding offers from our learning procedure.

196. Before diving in prediction models, we observed the change in the percentage of wins (2019 2023) depending on whether you are Amazon, FBA, or Merchant (6-month moving average).

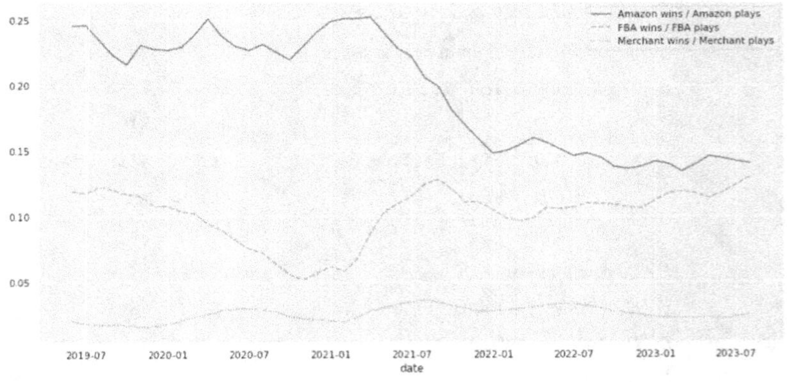

Figure 4: Change in percentage of wins, 2019-2023 depending on whether the seller is Amazon, FBA, or Merchant.

197. While this figure does not prove anything (all sellers could have changed their behaviour independently from the Buy Box), it helps describing the dataset depending on the category of the seller.

198. Additionally, we observe from July 2019 to July 2023 the variation in the percentage of times Amazon wins versus Amazon plays, by product family, over time.

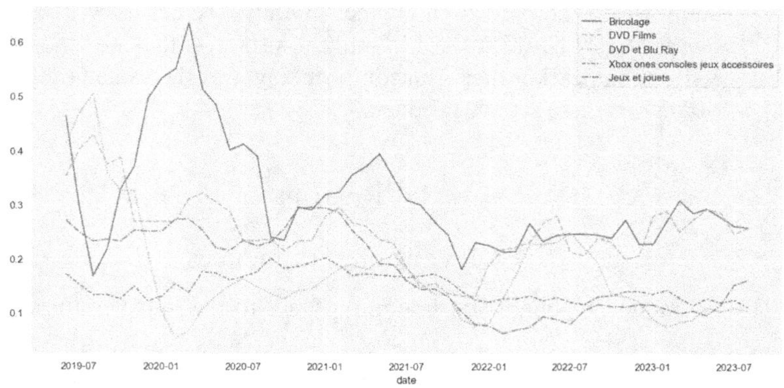

Figure 5: Variation in the percentage of times Amazon wins versus Amazon plays, by product family, over time.

3.3.3 Accuracy of the models' predictions

199. Overall, the four models proposed good to excellent prediction accuracies. About 83% accuracy for the "logit" model, which is very close to the results found in Raval (2023), about 90% for the "decision_tree" approach, 93% for the "random_forest" and 94% for the "gradient_boosting".

200. The figure bellow shows the respective accuracy of the four models for varying instances of the learning data sets (subtracting or adding samples in the learning data of the models).

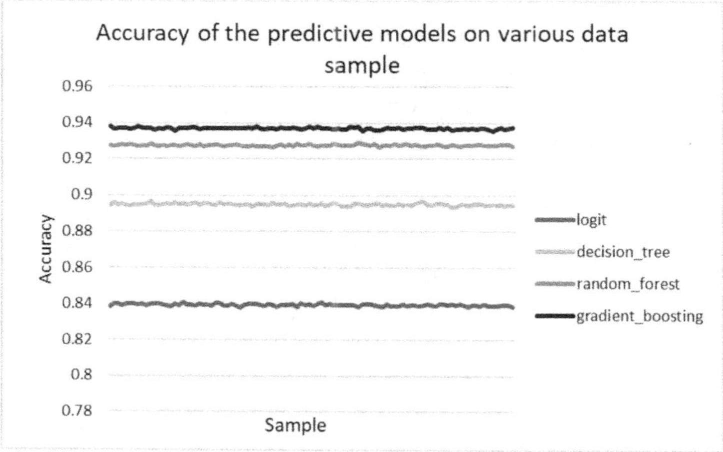

Figure 6: Accuracy of the predictive models on various data samples.

201. It is important to note that the four models are better at predicting the Buy Box winner when a product history is known. Previous winners offer a good indication of future winners, particularly when the competitor set is stable. A loss of about 2% performance occurs when a product is

unknown to the prediction engine. Funnily, the accuracy does not vary significatively between the 23 family of products that we studied, giving a strong indication that Amazon probably uses the same family of algorithms for these sets of products.

3.4 Results

3.4.1 Variables' influences

202. All models highlight a strong importance to the four variables:

- Price
- *isAmazon*
- isFBA
- allTimeRatingCount

203. For our best model, the "gradient_boosting", studying Shapley values is a classic way to observe the relative importance of the variables in the prediction. A prediction can be explained by considering that each feature value of the instance is a "player" in a game where the prediction is the payout. Shapley values – a method from coalitional game theory – tells us how to fairly distribute the "payout" among the features. The Shapley value is considered as one of the rare methods to deliver a full explanation because it is based on a solid theory and distributes the effects fairly (Shapley, 1953; Sundararajan and Najmi, 2020; Albini et al., 2023).

204. The Shapley values can, in theory, be computed for any kind of Machine Learning algorithm. We show the results on 1000 data points in Figure 8. Even if the (Shapley) value of a variable is hard to interpret (it represents its impact on the probability function of winning the Buy Box), their relative importance emphasizes their respective role in the classification model.

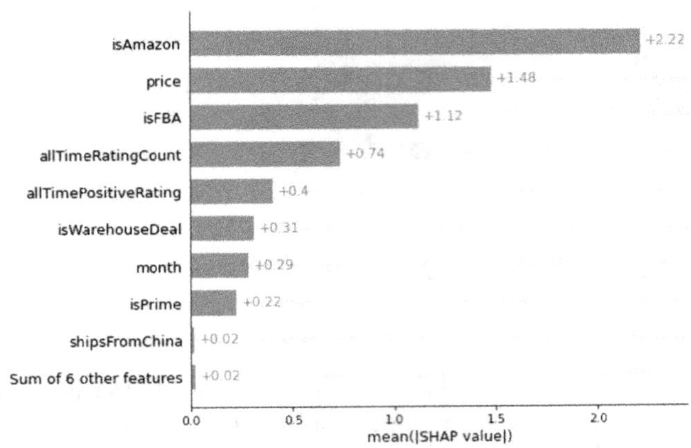

Figure 7: Shapley value computed on 1000 data points.

3.4.2 Differentiation event in the Buy Box's algorithm

205. From our model, can we detect a shift in the model over time, a tipping point?

206. We try to identify a change, relying on the hypothesis that Amazon started to make changes in the process of the negotiations of the commitments offered to the EU Commission. One of our hypotheses was to add "time" as a variable and to check if this variable plays a role in the explicability of the model. However, we are not sure that we will be able to identify a "clean break" over time in Amazon's algorithm. Indeed, on large platforms, A/B testing may be progressive, some family of products being privileged over others, in order to minimise risks and learn on the fly. This would make even more sense in the context of the commitments offered to the EU Commission since there were five months between the first set of commitment and the final set accepted by the EU Commission. Therefore, it might be challenging to identify a before and after the commitments over one day, but we expect to identify a shift in the model over two periods of time, amounting to several months.

207. The first insight on a change of "regime" for the Buy Box algorithm, is the change in chances of success of Amazon's offers, for every family of products as shown on figure 4.

208. For a given month m, say June 2022, our approach consisted in building two models. One model for all competitions happening before m, and another model for all competitions happening after m. We used the same gradient_boosting algorithm for the two models, with different learning data sets.

209. Three conclusions could be drawn:

   - first, the two models were of good to excellent quality, close to 92% accuracy,
   - applying the model_before to competitions after June 2022 (for which it had not been trained) gave significantly poorer accuracies, showing a strong difference in behaviour. A loss of 7% of accuracy was observed,
   - comparing Shapley values for the two models offered significant differences. The contribution of the variable *isAmazon* was considerably diminished in the model after June 2022 compared to the model before June 2022.

210. The figure highlights the change of importance of variable *isAmazon*, before and after June 2022.

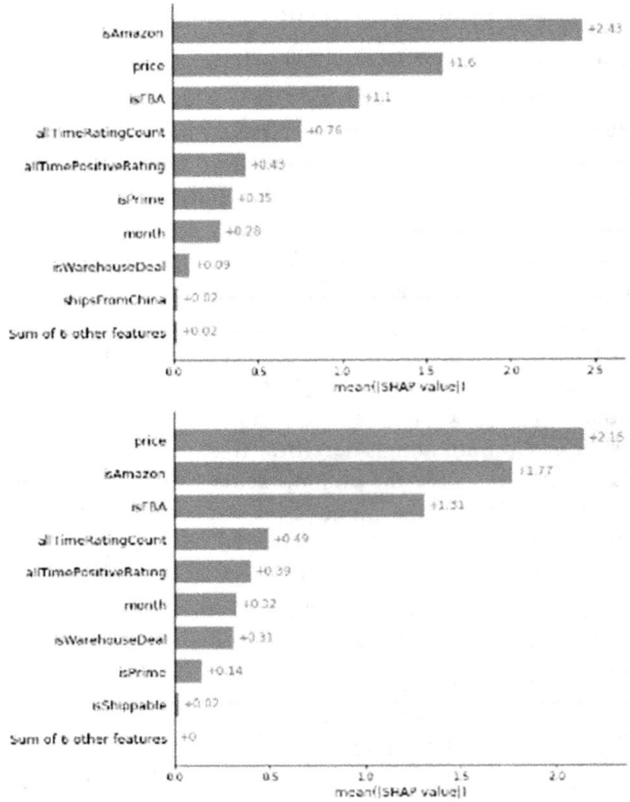

Figure 8 (above) and Figure 9 (below)
Figure 8: Shap values of the model before June 2022 (variable importance on the chance of winning).
Figure 9: Shap values of the model after June 2022 (variable importance on the chance of winning).

211. To summarise our results: we created a "surrogate model" that matches the behaviour of Amazon's Buy Box, and which is capable of reproducing the behaviour of the real Buy Box within 94% of accuracy. Our model, based on machine learning technology has learned from a sample of 1,600,000 seller 1 and seller 2 pairs, which one has the best chance to win the Buy Box for two given product offers. Our model showed even good results for a competition involving a completely unknown ASIN (without longitudinal learning).

212. When we analyse the explanatory variables in our model, relying on Shapley method, the variable *isAmazon* clearly stands out. The same result can be obtained with a logistic regression, but with a weaker predictive quality. When creating a counterfactual on the *isAmazon* variable, we observe a significant deterioration in the model's performance. The interpretation is the following. Our surrogate model replicates the real Amazon's Buy Box which needs the *isAmazon* variable to perform. It is possible that:

- Amazon uses variables other than those to which we have had access,
- The behaviour of Amazon as a seller, is so unique (by its pricing practice, its footprint or other selling tactics) that it can be inferred from the data without explicitly using the *isAmazon* variable, so we cannot be sure that the variable *isAmazon* is used,
- However, it does have an effect in our fairly precise model with the set of visible variables we had access to.

213. Finally, around mid-2022, we can observe a change in the model. The 'before' model (trained on competitions before June 2022) and the 'after' model (respectively) are not identical, not interchangeable, with different qualities in precision. The values of the explanatory variables (as defined by Shapley) are not the same before and after. In particular, the price variable (more important than before) and the *isAmazon* variable (less important than before). The impact of the counterfactual is significantly greater before than after. Furthermore, our descriptive analysis also shows that before mid-2022 Amazon won proportionately more competitions than after mid-2022.

214. This leads us to believe that Amazon heavily changed its algorithm during 2022 and that it seems that a similar algorithm is at work for all the product categories observed in our sample. The change occurred gradually because the effect of the change is not sudden and is identical for all categories observed (see Figure 5). Only looking at the variables available, Amazon products have an advantage over the competition, but this advantage has significantly decreased in the course of 2022.

3.5 Discussion and Policy implications

215. While it seems that the commitments had a positive effect, suggesting some efficiency, at which costs? In other words, what can our results say about the auditability of these commitments?

216. To obtain our results we first had to collect data through an API of a third party (which is costly and requires programming skills). This was only possible because of the fact that there are several API for Amazon, but this degree of data collection is not available for all online platforms that may be under antitrust scrutiny. The ideal situation would be for an auditor or a trustee to be able to "open the black box" and have access to both the data and the code. Since we could not have access to any of them, we relied on surrogate models. While the first one, a logistic regression, is rather simple, the machine learning models needed the expertise of data scientists. We chose to run four predictive models in order to compare the accuracy of each model from a simpler to a more sophisticated one. It would not be necessary for an auditor to run several models, however, their choice in

which model to rely on, would depend on a trade-off between the explicability of the model and its accuracy. In our research, the machine learnings models revealed a significantly higher degree of accuracy and sensitivity, supporting the need to have a cooperation of lawyers, economists, and data scientists on complex antitrust cases in digital markets.

217. From our results, around mid-2022, we can observe a change in the model. The 'before' model (trained on competitions before June 2022) and the 'after' model (respectively) are not identical, not interchangeable, with different qualities of precision. We made the hypothesis that the remedies should be implemented by the company on or around the date of implementation of the commitment decision. The remedies are supposed to restore competition from a situation in which, in this case, the company may have abused its dominance (since there is no formal decision on the finding). Since remedies are supposably correcting for a situation in which the firm is diverting profits and their implementation should cause a loss of profits, therefore the firm should delay as much as possible their implementation, i.e. 6 months from the date of the commitment decision. However, remedies are proposed in an information asymmetry setting, reinforced with the opacity of the algorithm of the Buy Box. Hence, when we observe a change in our model months before the date of the decision, it seems that the company is proposing remedies that they know they can implement, that they have already tested, suggesting the aim for the company to minimize their losses in their remedies' proposal. This minimization of the losses would consider the need that a trustee could observe a variation in the algorithm model, as an indication of compliance. Such a strategy could be questioned for *fairwashing*.[14]

218. While this observation could challenge whether a commitment decision was the right enforcement tool for this case, it is again necessary to recall that a commitment decision involves trade-offs. Commitment decision are cheaper and faster to implement (Dunne, 2014), and a systematic use of commitment decisions is optimal for the most harmful and difficult cases to deter (Choné et al., 2014). The Amazon's Buy Box would have unarguably been a difficult case to litigate, therefore a situation in which competition would have been restored under a formal infringement procedure could have taken years. However, the commitment decision comes at several costs (Wils, 2008; Steviev, 2014), including that, potential claims for damages from sellers on Amazon will be not able to rely on a formal infringement decision. All sellers that have been evicted or exploited, through these discriminatory practices, would need to demonstrate in Court that Amazon infringed competition law, establish the

14 Yaghini et al. (2024) illustrate the situation between a regulator wishing to design penalties that enforce compliance with their specification without disincentivizing machine learning builders from participation: they call it the regulation game for trustworthy machine learning. In their paper the authors model the relationship between machine learning builders and fairness and privacy regulators. They authors introduce ParetoPlay, acting as an equilibrium search algorithm, seeking social optimum solutions to the game.

causal link between the infringement and their damage, and evaluate the monetary damage.

219. Our model also triggers broader discussions in law & economics, among which the trade-off between the explicability of the methods chosen to assess the compliance of an algorithm and their accuracy. In our paper we compare the results of machine learning models, that are more sophisticated than a regression. However, the interpretation of the explanatory variables is not as straightforward than with a regression since we need to implement the Shapley method. If Shapley values have already been used as a presumption and are part of the state of art when it comes to machine learning models, it adds a degree of complexity in explaining the results while increasing the accuracy of the results. Hence, there is a clear trade-off between the explicability (which difficulty increases with the sophistication of the method) and the accuracy of the results (which, in our case, positively increases with the sophistication of the method). Which method is the most solid statistically to yield conclusions and self-preferencing prejudices? This question should be framed in the debate of what a proof is and what is the precision required for a technical proof advanced to a regulator. Should we be satisfied with a simple proof that is less explanatory, because it is easier to explain to a judge and therefore facilitates the regulatory discussion as well as the judicial review? Digital markets raise complex issues, making it more difficult to establish a counterfactual. There is a real need for technical expertise and inter-disciplinary dialogue between data scientists, lawyers, and economists (Fletcher et al., 2021). There is also the issue of the acceptance of AI-generated proofs in a context where AI applied to law seems to be poorly accepted and it is morally more complex to accept the risk of AI error, as opposed to a human error.

3.6 Conclusion

220. This paper aimed to provide a methodology for surrogate models in the frame of competition law commitments decision auditing algorithm. We relied on the Amazon's Buy Box case study. On the side of sellers, since Amazon is vertically integrated, the marketplace has an incentive to manipulate the ranking and engage into self-preferencing. In the case of the Amazon's Buy Box, the practice can either consist in preferencing Amazon, the seller, in the winning offers or, preferencing sellers subscribing to the FBA program (fulfilment by Amazon) since it also increases Amazon's profits. Therefore, if consumers are manipulated into purchasing products offered by the platform – because of the self-preferencing practices of the vertically integrated platform – complementors suffer from loss of profits. On one hand consumers are biased in their decision making by the recommender system and on the other hand the shift of demand

distorts the competition between suppliers (Fletcher et al.; 2023). In the EU Commission's commitment decision[15], the Commission expressed preliminary concerns that the anticompetitive practices involving the Buy Box "prejudices consumer choice and directly harms consumers by driving them to view and transact offers whose selection and display does not mirror the outcome of competition on the merits".[16]

221. We audited the commitment decision from the EU Commission in December 2022 to impose remedies on Amazon's Buy Box. We add to the literature both on the frame of our research, auditing an algorithm in the context of a commitment decision, as well as on the methodology, by complementing a logistical regression with more sophisticated machine learning methods.

222. Our results fit in the literature on product prominence in marketplaces, specifically when it comes to the Amazon's Buy Box. While previous papers studied the criteria to win the Buy Box, we add to the literature by testing four methods (logit, decision tree, random forest, gradient boosting) and by focusing on the compliance of Amazon with the commitment decision from the EU Commission. The choice of the categories in the dataset relied on a criterion of a minimum number of sellers for a same offer (at least 3), therefore, when we observe that the variable *isAmazon* contribution is diminished, it is not economically trivial. The more offers and sellers there are in our database, the greater the potential damage resulting from an infringement of competition law. Needless to also remind here that Amazon.fr is the most popular marketplace in France, with 312,36 million visits per month during the last semester of 2022.[17]

223. In this essay, we relied on a "surrogate model", to replicate the Buy Box algorithm. While our dataset only covers some categories on Amazon.fr, the large number of competitions allowed us to demonstrate, with a 94% accuracy, that the variable *isAmazon*, or variables correlated to it, had a positive effect on winning Buy Box before mid-2022, and that this positive effect has decreased after mid-2022. We can therefore conclude, from our model, on our limited data set, that being a product sold by Amazon was conferring an advantage and that this advantage has decreased. If it is not possible to state whether the change in the value of the variable *isAmazon* overtime can be interpretated such as Amazon stopping practices leading to unduly favouring its own services, it does seem that the commitments had a positive effect on the intra-marketplace competitions for the other sellers. However, the wording from the commitment decision, "non-discriminatory conditions", would suggest the need to establish a counterfactual, of what would non-discriminatory conditions

15 Antitrust procedure, article 9 Regulation (EC) 1/2003, case AT.40462 – Amazon marketplace and case AT.40703 – Amazon Buy Box, 20 December 2022.

16 Ibid, para 208.

17 Source is Statista: https://fr.statista.com/statistiques/475107/sites-e-commerce-les-plus-visites-france/.

mean compared to the situation in which discriminatory conditions were applied to select the featured offer. Regretfully, the commitment decision is opaque on the assessment of the effects of the compliance which rests in the hands of the designated trustee.

224. One of the limits of our models is the behavioural dimension that is not considered. Consumers are allowed to like and even prefer Amazon. If consumers like better Amazon, should not they benefit from the self-preferencing practices and aren't the complementors not efficient enough? This discussion can be framed on the very limited literature on the welfare effects of self-preferencing practices (Bougette et al., 2022). However, one could argue that consumers preferring Amazon products are not expressing a "real preference" but rather a shaped preference. Consumers or rather, algorithmic consumers[18] might have been trained to prefer Amazon's products. There would be a learning experience effect resulting in biased decision-making in favour of Amazon's products, which would not reflect a balancing of each qualitative dimension when purchasing a given product. While this strong hypothesis would need to be tested through an experiment, it would be aligned with the findings that AI has the potential to shape and manipulate consumers' preferences.

225. Finally, our paper fits in the discussion of all the other use cases of algorithms in antitrust. There is a strand in the empirical literature, in which data science techniques are relied upon to detect ex-post distortions on the market with massive datasets. Huber and Imhof (2019) as well as Wallimann et al. (2022) propose to combine statistical screens with machine learning techniques to detect bid-rigging cartels.

3.7 Bibliography

Albini, Emanuele, Shubham Sharma, Saumitra Mishra, Danial Dervovic, and Daniele Magazzeni. "On the Connection between Game-Theoretic Feature Attributions and Counterfactual Explanations." Proceedings of the 2023 AAAI/ACM Conference on AI, Ethics, and Society (2023):411-431.

Bertolini, Massimo, Davide Mezzogori, Mattia Neroni, and Francesco Zammori. "Machine Learning for Industrial Applications: A Comprehensive Literature Review." *Expert Systems with Applications* 175, (2021): 114820.

Bougette, Patrice, Oliver Budzinski, and Frédéric Marty. "Self-Preferencing and Competitive Damages: A Focus on Exploitative Abuses." *The Antitrust Bulletin* 67, no. 2 (2022): 190-207.

Breiman, Leo, Jerome Friedman, Charles J. Stone, and R. A. Olshen. *Classification and Regression Trees*. Taylor & Francis ed. (1984).

18 The expression "algorithmic consumers" comes from a paper from Gal and Elkin-Korren (2016) in which the authors emphasised both the virtues and downsides for consumers in relying on algorithms in their decision-making processes.

Breiman, Leo. "Bagging Predictors." *Machine Learning* 24, (1996): 123-140.

Breiman, Leo. "Random Forests." *Machine Learning* 45, (2001): 5-32.

Chen, Le, Alan Mislove, and Christo Wilson. "An Empirical Analysis of Algorithmic Pricing on Amazon Marketplace." Proceedings of the 25th international conference on World Wide Web (2016):1339-1349.

Chen, Tianqi and Carlos Guestrin. "Xgboost: A Scalable Tree Boosting System." Proceedings of the 22nd ACM sigkdd international conference on knowledge discovery and data mining. (2016):785-794.

Choné, Philippe, Saïd Souam, and Arnold Vialfont. "On the Optimal use of Commitment Decisions Under European Competition Law." *International Review of Law and Economics* 37, (2014): 169-179.

Cure, Morgane, Matthias Hunold, Reinhold Kesler, Ulrich Laitenberger, and Thomas Larrieu. "Vertical Integration of Platforms and Product Prominence." *Quantitative Marketing and Economics* 20, no. 4 (2022): 353-395.

Etro, Federico. "The Economics of Amazon." *Available at SSRN 4307213* (2022).

Etumnu, Chinonso E. "A Competitive Marketplace Or an Unfair Competitor? an Analysis of Amazon and its Best Sellers Ranks." *Journal of Agricultural Economics* 73, no. 3 (2022): 924-937.

Farronato, Chiara, Andrey Fradkin, and Alexander MacKay. "Self-Preferencing at Amazon: Evidence from Search Rankings." *NBER Working Paper 30894,* January, 2023. doi:10.3386/w30894. https://www.nber.org/papers/w30894.

Feasey, Richard and Jan Krämer. *Implementing Effective Remedies for Anti-Competitive Intermediation Bias on Vertically Integrated Platforms* Centre on Regulation in Europe asbl (CERRE), 2019.

Fletcher, Amelia, Gregory S. Crawford, Jacques Crémer, David Dinielli, Paul Heidhues, Michael Luca, Tobias Salz, Monika Schnitzer, Fiona M. Scott Morton, and Katja Seim. "Consumer Protection for Online Markets and Large Digital Platforms." *Available at SSRN 3923588* (2021).

Fletcher, Amelia, Peter Ormosi, and Rahul Savani. "Recommender Systems and Supplier Competition on Platforms." *Journal of Competition Law & Economics* (2023). doi:https://doi.org/10.1093/joclec/nhad009.

Friedman, Jerome H. "Greedy Function Approximation: A Gradient Boosting Machine." *Annals of Statistics* (2001): 1189-1232.

Fry Chantal and Manna Sukanya. "Can We Group Similar Amazon Reviews: A Case Study with Different Clustering Algorithms" *2016 IEEE Tenth International Conference on Semantic Computing (ICSC)*, Laguna Hills, CA, USA, 2016, pp. 374-377, doi: 10.1109/ICSC.2016.71.

Gaddis, S. M. (2018). Audit studies: Behind the scenes with theory, method, and nuance. Vol. 14. Springer.

Gal, Michal S. and Nicolas Petit. "Radical Restorative Remedies for Digital Markets." *Berkeley Tech.LJ* 36, (2021): 617.

Gautier, Axel and Nicolas Petit. "Optimal Enforcement of Competition Policy: The Commitments Procedure Under Uncertainty." *European Journal of Law and Economics* 45, (2018): 195-224.

Gómez-Losada, Álvaro and Néstor Duch-Brown. "Competing for Amazon's Buy Box: A Machine-Learning Approach." Springer, 2019.

Gómez-Losada, Álvaro, Gualberto Asencio-Cortés, and Néstor Duch-Brown. "Automatic Eligibility of Sellers in an Online Marketplace: A Case Study of Amazon Algorithm." *Information* 13, no. 2 (2022): 44.

Grinsztajn, Léo, Edouard Oyallon, and Gaël Varoquaux. "Why do Tree-Based Models Still Outperform Deep Learning on Typical Tabular Data?" *Advances in Neural Information Processing Systems* 35, (2022): 507-520.

Hoehn. "Challenges in designing and implementing remedies in innovation intensive industries and the digital economy." In Gerard, Damien and Assimakis Komninos. *Remedies in EU Competition Law: Substance, Process and Policy* Kluwer Law International (2020).

Huber, Martin; Imhof, David. "Machine learning with screens for detecting bid-rigging cartels." *International Journal of Industrial Organization* Vol. 65 (2019).

Hunold, Matthias, Ulrich Laitenberger, and Guillaume Thébaudin. "Bye-Box: An Analysis of Non-Promotion on the Amazon Marketplace." *CRED WORKING PAPER no 2022-4* (2022).

Janger, Edward J. and Aaron D. Twerski. "The Heavy Hand of Amazon: A Seller Not a Neutral Platform." *Brook.J.Corp.Fin.& Com.L.* 14, (2019): 259.

Marty, Frédéric and Reis, Patrice. "Perspectives juridiques et économiques sur les procédures négociées en droit de la concurrence." *SciencePo Working papers* Main hal-00614942, HAL. (2011)

Metaxa, Danaë, Joon Sung Park, Ronald E. Robertson, Karrie Karahalios, Christo Wilson, Jeff Hancock and Christian Sandvig (2021), "Auditing Algorithms", Foundations and Trends® in Human-Computer Interaction: Vol. 14, No. 4, pp 272–344. DOI: 10.1561/1100000083.

Mullainathan, S., M. Noeth, and A. Schoar. (2012). "The market for financial advice: An audit study." Tech. rep. National Bureau of Economic Research.

OECD. *Remedies and Commitments in Abuse Cases.* OECD Competition Policy Roundtable Background Note (2022).

Policarpo, Lucas Micol, Diórgenes Eugênio da Silveira, Rodrigo da Rosa Righi, Rodolfo Antunes Stoffel, Cristiano André da Costa, Jorge Luis Victoria Barbosa, Rodrigo Scorsatto, and Tanuj Arcot. "Machine Learning through the Lens of E-Commerce Initiatives: An Up-to-Date Systematic Literature Review." *Computer Science Review* 41, (2021): 100414.

Prokhorenkova, Liudmila, Gleb Gusev, Aleksandr Vorobev, Anna Veronika Dorogush, and Andrey Gulin. "CatBoost: Unbiased Boosting with Categorical Features." *Advances in Neural Information Processing Systems* 31, (2018).

Raval, Devesh. "Steering in One Click: Platform Self-Preferencing in the Amazon Buy Box." (2023) https://deveshraval.github.io/buyBox.pdf

Seele Peter, Dierksmeier Claus, Hofstetter, Reto *et al.* "Mapping the Ethicality of Algorithmic Pricing: A Review of Dynamic and Personalized Pricing." *J Bus Ethics* 170, 697–719 (2021). https://doi.org/10.1007/s10551-019-04371-w

Shapley, Lloyd S. *A Value for N-Person Games. Contributions to the Theory of Games.* (1953).

Shwartz-Ziv, Ravid and Amitai Armon. "Tabular Data: Deep Learning is Not all You Need." *Information Fusion* 81, (2022): 84-90.

Maitra, Subhradeep, Laxminarayan Sahoo, and Kalishankar Tiwary. 2022. "Study, Analysis and Comparison Between Amazon A10 and A11 Search Algorithm". *Journal of Computer Science Research* 4 (4):1-6. https://doi.org/10.30564/jcsr.v4i4.5111.

Sundararajan, Mukund and Amir Najmi. "The Many Shapley Values for Model Explanation." *Proceedings of the 37th International Conference on Machine Learning* (2020).

Waldfogel, Joel. Amazon Self-preferencing in the Shadow of the Digital Markets Act. No. w32299. National Bureau of Economic Research, 2024.

Wallimann, Hannes; Imohf, David; Huber, Martin. "A Machine Learning Approach for Flagging Incomplete Bid-Rigging Cartels." *Comput Econ* 62, 1669–1720 (2023). https://doi.org/10.1007/s10614-022-10315-w

Wils, Wouter PJ. "Settlements of EU Antitrust Investigations: Commitment Decisions Under Article 9 of Regulation no. 1/2003." *World Competition* 29, no. 3 (2006).

Wils, Wouter PJ. "Ten Years of Regulation 1/2003-a Retrospective." *Journal of European Competition Law & Practice* 4, no. 4 (2013): 293-301.

Yaghini, Mohammad; Liu, Patty; Boenisch, Franziska; Papernot, Nicolas. "Regulation Games for Trustworthy Machine Learning". (2024) https://arxiv.org/abs/2402.03540

GENERAL CONCLUSION

226. This dissertation dealt with the compensation, prevention, and remediation of a competitive damage, with different perspectives and tools, combining methods from data analysis, econometrics, and game theory. Each essay answered a research question under different angles of economics of litigation studying unilateral conducts from a dominant player causing a competitive damage. The general aim of the dissertation was to compare the benefits and hurdles of complementary tools to traditional public enforcement of competition law in digital markets.

227. The first essay delineated the determinants of a successful EU competition law damages action following an abuse of dominance, running a logistical regression on a dataset of 194 damages cases in France, Italy, and UK. The results were discussed against the on-going and upcoming private enforcement actions in the digital markets. The second essay explored, with a Hotelling game theory model, whether Article 5(4) of the DMA could incentivize gatekeepers to adapt their business model and whether the business users would benefit and/or also modify their own business model. The third essay audited the ranking strategy of the algorithm of an online platform, via data scraping on a price tracker, after a commitment decision from the EU Commission, and relied on four models, including machine learning techniques (logistical regression, decision tree, random forest, gradient boosting).

228. In the context of a global enforcement system strategy aiming to deter unilateral conducts in digital markets, this dissertation analysed the effectiveness of compensation through private enforcement of competition law, remediation through the *ex-ante* rules of the DMA, and prevention of a competitive damage through competition law commitment decisions.

229. The research question of the first essay was the following: what are the determinants of successful damages actions following an abuse of dominance?

230. Contrary to previous studies mapping damages actions following infringements of Article 101 TFEU, the results indicate that follow-on actions relating to abuse of dominance under Article 102 TFEU are associated with a lower likelihood of success than stand-alone actions. This finding points to differences in the litigation of damages actions between infringements of Articles 101 and 102 TFEU. No clear association is identified between the type of relief sought and the outcome of damages actions. This may reflect the fact that, for claimants, seeking injunctive relief and claiming monetary damages are not mutually exclusive strategies. The introduction of the Damages Directive and its transposition are positively and statistically associated with successful outcomes in damages actions. With respect to economic sectors, claims brought in the information and

communication sector and in the transport sector are associated with a lower likelihood of success compared to claims in other sectors included in the database. When considering whether sectoral case concentration, used as a proxy for a potential learning effect, is related to case outcomes, the estimated association differs across jurisdictions: the likelihood of success is higher for damages cases in France but lower for damages cases in Italy. Finally, with regard to the digital sector, claims introduced in this sector are associated with a lower likelihood of success, this result is more pronounced in Italy. However, when interacting the digital sector variable with the log-linearised amount of damages, the interaction term is positive and statistically significant, suggesting that the relationship between digital-sector claims and case outcomes may depend on the scale of the damages sought.

231. The results of the first essay were put in perspective with the analysis of the on-going private enforcement actions in the database following the Google Shopping case. While there is not yet a final decision, several difficulties have already arisen for victims of the abuse of dominance when introducing claim for damages. First, the Google Shopping case started following the opening of a formal investigation by the EU Commission in 2010, therefore, considering the duration of the public enforcement case, only "exploited" companies, still on the market, with the necessary financial resources can bring claims. Furthermore, in the on-going private enforcements cases in the UK, Italy, and France, Google have tried opposing several arguments to delay or fragment claims for damages, such as raising lack of jurisdiction or arguing against access to documents.

232. Damages actions for competition law infringements were first designed for follow-on actions for infringements to Article 101 TFEU, since, at the time of the inception of the Directive, cartel infringements were deemed the most harmful. Therefore, this essay brought light both on the determinants of the under-studied claims for damages following an abuse of dominance, and more specifically, on the on-going and upcoming claims for damages following abuse of dominance in the digital sectors considering both the global enforcement effort and the potential widespread damage that can result from the anticompetitive behaviours of the dominant players in digital markets.

233. The difficulties in researching this first essay mainly resided in the collection of cases. The lack of harmonised and official sources with a clear identification of the private enforcement cases for abuse of dominance also require relying on several sources and crossing information collected, especially since the database counts cases and not decisions. In some events, older case law was identified, but it was not possible to find a copy of the judgment. There was also some heterogeneity in the writing of judgments, for example, some judgments would not mention the original amount of monetary damages requested or would not differentiate the final amount

from the interests received. This heterogeneity also prevented the collection of more granular data. For example, abusive practices can be divided between exclusionary or exploitative practices and then sub-categorised as specific types of unilateral practices. While there is no finite list characterizing unilateral practices, it was possible, for exclusionary practices, to rely on the EU Commission guidance documents from 2008 in applying Article 82 of the EC Treaty to abusive exclusionary conduct. An attempt was made to categorize cases first between exploitative and exclusionary and then by sub-categories of abuses (for example: tying, refusal to deal, predation, discriminatory practices, excessive pricing). However, it would have been mostly deducted from the facts of the case, since in the vast majority of case law, the judge does not expressly refer to the abuse for being exclusionary or exploitative. Regarding the attempt of linking each case by with a sub-category of unilateral practices, taking the example of the damages cases initiated in France in the database, in 27 cases there were at least two sub-categories of abuses relied upon in the decisions, in 10 cases there were three or more than three sub-categories of abuses relied upon in the decisions. Therefore, linking a case to only one sub-category of abusive practice would have required selection.

234. The main limits from this essay were the limited number of cases (194 cases from three countries) and the lack of more granular data. For example, it would have been interesting to collect and compare methodologies of quantification of damages in each case, however, only few judgments explicitly state the economic analysis behind the quantum of damages.

235. While it seems unlikely, in the context of predictive justice, to build a strong predictive model considering the heterogeneity of the case law of claims for damages, it would be relevant to expand the data collection in more countries, collecting data on a more granular level, and expanding the analysis on whether claims for damages are indeed harmonised in the EU. This project, of building an EU wide database of private enforcement cases for infringements to competition law, is under discussion with Prof. Hornkohl (University of Vienna).

236. From compensation to remediation, the research question of the second essay was the following: Does Art 5(4) of the DMA incentivize gatekeepers to adapt their business model and do business users benefit and/or also modify their own business model?

237. The second essay was co-authored with Christian Rusche. From a game theory model, our results show that the introduction of the prohibition of anti-steering clauses in the DMA may result in the following effects:

   (a) Using the platform becomes more attractive to business users.

   (b) The obligation is also attractive and, therefore, business users make use of it. To do so, they might even open up an independent web shop.

(c) The platform has an incentive to become vertically integrated.

(d) The amount of data available for business users and the platform is likely to increase.

(e) Following the introduction of the obligation, fees are likely to increase if all business users were already using the platform before. Otherwise, the effect of the obligation on the amount of the fee is indeterminate and depends on the specific manifestation of the variables.

238. Since publishing this essay,[1] there have been some developments in relation to anti-steering clauses in competition law and under the DMA. First, on the 4th of March 2024, the EU Commission fined Apple 1.8 billion euros for banning "music streaming app developers from fully informing iOS users about alternative and cheaper music subscription services available outside of the app and from providing any instructions about how to subscribe to such offers".[2] The press release stressed that the conduct lasted for more than ten years, leading to monetary and non-monetary harm on iOS users. Furthermore, the designated gatekeepers under the DMA in September 2023, had to comply with all obligations of the DMA since the 7th of March, including the anti-steering clause prohibition. Each gatekeeper also had the obligation to provide the Commission with a non-confidential summary of the compliance report (Article 11 of the DMA). On the 25th of March 2024, the EU Commission opened an investigation to assess whether the measures implemented by Alphabet and Apple were compliant with Article 5(4) of the DMA, which requires gatekeepers to allow app developers to "steer" consumers to offers outside the gatekeepers' app stores, free of charge.[3] In the press release, the Commission expressed concerns that the measures proposed by Alphabet and Apple may not be fully compliant, as they impose various restrictions and limitations, among which, constraining, developers' ability to freely communicate and promote offers and directly conclude contracts, including by imposing various charges.

239. The early stage of this research, conducted pre-enforcement period of the DMA, explains its exploratory nature, which was constrained by a limited economics literature on anti-steering clauses, and more broadly, studying the potential effects of the DMA.

240. To go further, while this essay tried to study theoretically the consequences of the introduction of the obligation, it would be now possible to confront these results with a more practical approach, comparing the effects of the DMA compliance proposals by the gatekeepers with a simulation model.

1 European Journal of Law & Economics in October 2023.

2 Press release: https://ec.europa.eu/commission/presscorner/detail/en/ip_24_1161

3 Press release: https://ec.europa.eu/commission/presscorner/detail/en/ip_24_1689

In continuing this research, it would be relevant to question whether the Hotelling model would still prevail, and which simulation models could be relied upon. We chose the Hotelling model, fitting in the literature which already relied on the Hotelling model when modeling firms' interactions in two-sided markets (Spulber, 1999; Alexandrov et al., 2011). Even closer to our paper, Decarolis and Li (2023) study the Google Android case and rely on a Hotelling model to demonstrate how the enforcement of these dimensions can result in a greater impact in the online search engine markets, increasing the number of potential users of competing search engines. However, the Hotelling model is not the only one that was relied upon in economic research in digital markets. Ganuza and Llobet (2018), in their book shedding light on the economic analysis and the digital revolution, review the work of Haan, Moraga-Gonzalez et Petrikaité (2017) building on the Wolinsky framework and the one of Anderson and Renault (2017), in which they modify the framework of Wolinsky (1986), Anderson and Renault (1999) and use Weitzman (1979). Finally, we could expand and complete this essay with a numerical simulation, taking the example of the paper from Bougette and Charlier (2015) in which they complete the results of their model with a numerical simulation on the effects of feed-in-tariffs programs in the domain of the renewable electricity.

241. Finally, from remediation to prevention, the research question of the third essay was the following: is it possible to audit the ranking strategy of the algorithm of an online platform, via data scraping on a price tracker and machine learning?

242. The third essay was co-authored with Benoît Rottembourg. Our results show good to excellent prediction accuracies on the four models, from about 83% accuracy for the logit model to 94% accuracy for the gradient boosting model. Relying on machine learning technology, we created a "surrogate model" that matches the behaviour of Amazon's Buy Box and that has learned from a sample of 1,600,000 seller 1 and seller 2 pairs, which one has the best chance to win the Buy Box. When we analyse the explanatory variables in our model, relying on Shapley method, the variable *isAmazon* clearly stands out. The same result can be obtained with a logistic regression, but with a weaker predictive quality. When we tried to identify a change, relying on the hypothesis that Amazon complied with the commitments offered to the EU Commission, we can observe a change in the model around mid-2022. The 'before' model (trained on competitions before June 2022) and the 'after' model (respectively) are neither identical nor interchangeable, with different qualities of precision. The values of the explanatory variables (as defined by Shapley) are not the same before and after. In particular, the price variable is more important than before and the *isAmazon* variable is less important than before. Furthermore, our descriptive analysis also shows that before mid-2022 Amazon won proportionately more competitions than after mid-2022.

This leads us to believe that Amazon heavily changed its algorithm during 2022 and that it seems that a similar algorithm is at work for all the product categories observed in our sample. The change occurred gradually because the effect of the change is not sudden and is identical for all categories observed. Only looking at the variables available, Amazon products have an advantage over the competition, but this advantage has significantly decreased in the course of 2022.

243. Since researching this essay, Waldfogel (2024) studied the changes in Amazon's own products in the ranking of Amazon search results following the introduction of the DMA. Waldfogel used data on 8 million Amazon search results on 22 Amazon domains between June 2023 and March 2024 and found that after the EU designated Amazon a "gatekeeper" platform in September 2023, the Amazon rank differential fell from a 30-position advantage to a 20-position advantage, and that the change of Amazon search rankings appeared in both Europe and other jurisdictions.

244. While researching on the topic, the main difficulty we face was in the choice of the angle of research between experimental economics or data analysis. It would also have been possible to research this topic under different perspectives.

245. To include a behavioural dimension, we could have created a fake recommendation system, making assumptions about customers' behaviours inspired by real-life situations and simulating the effects to validate scenarios. In which case, we could have relied on discrete choice modelling. For example, Feldman et al. (2022) compare the performances of two approaches to predict customers' behaviour. The authors rely on historical data from two marketplaces from Alibaba with the aim of finding the optimal set of products to display to customers landing on these marketplaces. On one hand they use a machine learning algorithm to estimate the purchase probabilities for the customer, on the other hand they use a multinomial logit model (MNL) to predict purchasing probabilities for each arriving customer. In this specific case, while the logit model is simple, it was designed to capture consumers' behaviours and account for substitution patterns. The authors find that fitter machine learning models produce more accurate results than the MNL, but the MNL approach generates higher revenue per visit. The authors demonstrated, with their experiment on Alibaba, that MNL models in product recommendation systems have the potential to outperform machine learning models.

246. In terms of limits in this essay, we relied on a surrogate model, with data collected from a third-party Amazon API. Therefore, not only we do not have access to all the variables of the algorithms, but we do not know its optimisation functions either. We were in a situation that was even more constrained than an auditor which should have access to all the data and information required.

247. To go further, the following step of this paper would be to compute the prejudice for the sellers caused by Amazon's self-preferencing practices. While the remedies allow for a faster legal action, preventing a potential damage from lasting, victims cannot rely on a decision for a follow-on damages action. Hence, any seller harmed by Buy Box's algorithm would need to establish Amazon's infringement under Article 102 TFEU, the causal link between the infringement and their prejudice, and quantify the damage. The aim of compensating for the harm suffered in competition law is to replace the injured party in the situation that would have prevailed should the infringement have not taken place. In order to quantify the harm suffered by the other sellers on Amazon's marketplace by self-preferencing practices, it would be necessary to compare the period of the alleged infringement with a hypothetical situation, namely a counterfactual, of what would have happened should the infringement have not occurred. We expect the need to build at least two counterfactuals. First, as a potential volume effect in the quantified harm, we would compare the situation of the sellers losing the Buy Box with a counterfactual of what would have been their sales should self-preferencing practices have not occurred. Second, as potential price affects the quantified harm, we would compare the situation of the sellers winning the Buy Box with a counterfactual of what would have been the price at which they would have won the Buy Box should self-preferencing practices have not occurred.

248. To conclude, this dissertation relied on different methods and demonstrated in the first essay the singularity of the determinants of a successful claim for damages following an infringement to Article 102 TFEU compared to an infringement to Article 101 TFEU. The econometrics analysis on case analysis demonstrated the specific difficulties faced by claimants in the digital sector. The second essay, in the context of the ex-ante remediation of economic damages in digital sectors, took the example of the anti-steering prohibition in the DMA to demonstrate, with a game theory model, the shift of incentives and potential effects on the market. Finally, the third essay, in the context of preventing a competitive damage in digital markets, took the example of a commitment decision imposed on Amazon, to demonstrate, with data analysis, the added value for the auditor of relying on machine learning technologies in an information asymmetry setting, due to the nature of commitments decisions and the opacity of algorithms.

249. The general aim of the dissertation was to compare the benefits and hurdles of complementary tools to traditional public enforcement of competition law in digital markets. This dissertation argues that prohibition decisions in competition law (Article 7, Regulation 1/2003) benefit from being complemented by alternative enforcement methods to ensure the deterrence of unilateral practices in digital markets. While there were indeed some lessons to be drawn from the determinants of a successful private enforcement

action following an abuse of dominance, the case analysis showed that there are additional specific difficulties that will need to be overcome in digital markets (including but not limited to the attempt from undertakings to fragment widespread damages claims and the difficulties in quantifying damages for claimants). The DMA is expected to shift incentives on the digital markets and increase their contestability. However, from theory to practice, gatekeepers might be reluctant to give up their long-earned undue profits, which in turn, might trigger further enforcement efforts. Commitments are the fast-track procedure in competition law, if they prevent the damage from lasting (in comparison to lengthy public enforcement), but they are only worth it if the commitments correct the anticompetitive behaviours and can be effectively monitored. When it comes to digital markets and opaque algorithms, the design and monitoring of remedies will require working hand in hand with data scientists.

250. Although there are some benefits (but also hurdles) to private enforcement of competition law, the *ex-ante* rules of the DMA as well as commitments decisions, these instruments complement the public enforcement of competition law and cannot act as substitutes. Private enforcement does not aim to deter but to compensate (though it can have deterring effects). The DMA prohibits a finite list of practices and does not cover all anti-competitive behaviours. Finally, commitments decisions should not be used in every case, otherwise no liability would ever be established. Hence, this dissertation recommends a parallel enforcement of competition law (through the lenses of public enforcement, commitments decisions and private enforcements) with sector-specific regulations such as the DMA.

251. To conclude, this dissertation aims to be a first step in analysing the instruments available to the regulators and private parties in deterring unilateral practices in digital markets. It would be relevant to pursue the analysis of the interplay of competition law with additional digital-sector specific regulations, even when they do not target anticompetitive behaviours, to assess whether their enforcement could affect the digital markets structures and create incentives to compete.

BIBLIOGRAPHY

Alexandrov, Alexei, George Deltas, and Daniel F. Spulber. "Antitrust and competition in two-sided markets." *Journal of Competition Law and Economics* 7, no. 4 (2011): 775-812.

Bougette, Patrice, and Christophe Charlier. "Renewable energy, subsidies, and the WTO: Where has the 'green'gone?" *Energy Economics* 51 (2015): 407-416.

Decarolis, Francesco and Muxin Li. "Regulating online search in the EU: from the Android case to the Digital Markets Act and Digital Services Act." *International Journal of Industrial Organization* 90, (2023): 102983.

Feldman, Jacob, et al. "Customer choice models vs. machine learning: Finding optimal product displays on Alibaba." *Operations Research* 70.1 (2022): 309-328.

González, José L. Moraga. "Consumer search in digital markets." *Economic analysis of the digital revolution* (2018): 181.

Spulber, Daniel F. *Market Microstructure: Intermediaries and the Theory of the Firm* Cambridge University Press, 1999.

Waldfogel, Joel. "Amazon self-preferencing in the shadow of the Digital Markets Act." *National Bureau of Economic Research* (2024) No. w32299.

ACKNOWLEDGEMENTS

252. I would like to start by thanking Professor Christophe Hurlin for showing me the way from Law to Economics and for being an incredible source of motivation and mentoring during these past years – proving that sometimes all can happen in life by complaining like a French person while working in a supermarket. It is thanks to Professor Hurlin that I sent my application to the Master Degree *Economie du Droit* in the University of Nanterre. Before my Master's Degree, I was only a lawyer by training with an interest in Economics, an outsider. Therefore, I am thankful to Professor Langlais for betting on me. These two years were rich and intense thanks to all the professors and my classmates. During the Master's Degree, I had the chance to attend the competition law class from Professor Ludovic Bernardeau, who put me in contact with my -not yet- PhD supervisor, as he recommended: "you should talk to him about your research".

253. Special thanks to Professor Saïd Souam, who is obviously the best, but we already knew that. He led my first steps in research, from my Master's Degree Thesis to our first publication, with his kind encouragements and advice all along the Ph.D research. A sense of rigour, an ocean of knowledge but above all a generosity and an inspiring human approach to teaching and research. Thank you for never letting a student leave the class without fully grasping the concepts (and sorry for the extra hours).

254. While finishing my Master Degree, I had the opportunity to join Concurrences where I was fully immersed in the latest case law in competition and antitrust around the world. It felt special to win this PhD Award from Concurrences and to work together on the publication. I would like to thank the members of the jury for honouring me with their trust by awarding me the Concurrences PhD Award. Thank you to Professors Emmanuel Combe, Marc Bourreau, Griet Jans and Constance Monnier-Schlumberger. I conducted my research and wrote this thesis while reading your work. Thank you for being a source of inspiration and academic rigour. I have a special thought for Guillaume Thébaudin, last year's Concurrences PhD Award winner and a very dear friend from our shared DMA enforcement days.

255. I was lucky to spend most of my PhD research while working at the College of Europe. I would like to thank the whole Economics Department, their professors, with a special thought for the professors and students from the European Law and Economic Analysis option. The ELEA option helped me keep a foot in Law. Therefore, I would like to thank Professor Govaere and Professor Garben for including me in the life of the European Law Department and their support for my PhD research. In the European

Economics Department of the College of Europe, I would like to thank Professor Peter Claeys for his guidance and support for my research.

256. The College of Europe was a big family, so I am grateful for all the colleagues who welcomed me with open harms, those who supported me during these years of research, and those who are now friends: Tony O'Connor, Claire Soupart, Julien Tribout (also for being Vanille's official cat sitter), Georgia Theodorakopoulou, Jonas Corneille, Roselien Van Loocke, Alvaro Martin Moran and Anis Issa.

257. Finally, having written two-thirds of this thesis on self-preferencing audits and anti-steering clauses, there came a point when I simply had to switch sides. It is thanks to the College of Europe that I had the chance to meet my boss, and it is a great joy to be surrounded by brilliant colleagues in the European Commission's DMA team, and to work with inspiring and encouraging leaders: Rita Wezenbeek, Filomena Chirico, Denis Sparas, Luca Aguzzoni, and Sophie Ahlswede.

258. To all the colleagues in academia, to all the academic events and conferences during which I met and learned from inspiring academics, from Brazil to Germany. To those colleagues who always give you a word of encouragement before and after presenting your paper, to those who ask the right questions to push you to improve your research and to those who clearly have a better talent at communicating on social media and will not give up until you start doing the same (Alba Ribera Martínez, you know I'm talking about you). To this incredible community of brilliant young researchers who support each other and understand what we are going through, to Dr. Léna Hornkhol and to the others: thank you.

259. Members of my thesis Committee, Professor Bougette and Professor Sinclair-Desgagné, and members of the GREDEG: thank you for your guidance and support. I have special thoughts here for Ilona Dielen: you are an amazing teacher and researcher. And Nathalie, my PhD partner, it is your turn now.

260. I am thankful to Christian Rusche and Benoît Rottembourg for co-authoring the second and third chapter of this dissertation. I have learned so much by your sides and you have made co-authoring an easy and nerdy-fun experience. Vanille misses our video calls.

261. I could not have imagined better supervision conditions for my PhD. I am forever grateful to my PhD Supervisor, Frédéric Marty. First, for convincing me to do a PhD and for providing his PhD students with a network of present, past, and potential future PhD students in which we could connect and support one and other. Thank you for inspiring a vocation and answering countless emails and messages, but most of all, thank you for acknowledging the doubts I may have had, for letting me be my true-very-honest-self all along the PhD and for setting the bar so high for what it means to be both a brilliant and mindful academic that

I will now take me a lifetime to reach it. I have been lucky to write my PhD under your supervision and it has been an honour to learn from you. *Et qu'on se le dise, le poids d'une thèse de doctorat s'adoucit avec un directeur de thèse qui a l'accent du sud.*

262. Polina. My best friend. Words are not enough. Thank you for everything. You were there for me at every step along the way, from when I was too motivated from my own good to when it was harder to do it all. I am glad I finished the PhD and have not succumbed to heading for the mountains to make goat cheese as we both know I would have sucked at it. I could not have done the PhD without you. You are the best human being I know.

Vanille, oui, tu es dans les remerciements, arrête de miauler.

À ma famille, de l'Auvergne au Doctorat, il semblait y avoir un monde entre les deux, votre soutien en était le pont. Merci d'avoir toujours essayé de comprendre ce que je pouvais bien faire à tout le temps travailler sur mon ordi alors que vraiment je ne vous facilitais pas la tâche de passer du droit à l'économie. Merci pour nos weekends et nos vacances en famille, de m'avoir fait ralentir quand j'avais du mal à maintenir l'équilibre. Tonton, je suis désolée, mais je ne suis toujours pas avocate !

La gloire de mon père. Papa, Merci de toujours croire en moi.

Concurrences
Competition Laws Review

Concurrences Review

Concurrences is a print and online quarterly peer reviewed journal dedicated to EU and national competitions laws. It has been launched in 2004 as the flagship of the Institute of Competition Law in order to provide a forum for academics, practitioners and enforcers. Concurrences' influence and expertise has garnered contributions or interviews with such figures as Christine Lagarde, Bill Kovacic, Emmanuel Macron, Antonin Scalia and Magrethe Vestager.

Contents

More than 15,000 articles, print and/or online. Quarterly issues provide current coverage with contributions from the EU or national or foreign countries thanks to more than 2,500 authors in Europe and abroad.

Format

In order to balance academic contributions with opinions or legal practice notes, Concurrences provides its insight and analysis in a number of formats:

- Forewords: Opinions by leading academics or enforcers
- Interviews: Interviews of antitrust experts
- On-Topics: 4 to 6 short papers on hot issues
- Law & Economics: Short papers written by economists for a legal audience
- Articles: Long academic papers
- Case Summaries: Case commentary on EU and French case law
- Legal Practice: Short papers for in-house counsels
- International: Medium size papers on international policies
- Books Review: Summaries of recent antitrust books
- Articles Review: Summaries of leading articles published in 45 antitrust journals

Boards

The Scientific Committee is headed by Laurence Idot, Professor at Panthéon Assas University. The International Committee is headed by Frederic Jenny, OECD Competition Comitteee Chairman. Boards members include Douglas Ginsburg, Benoît Cœuré, Howard Shelanski, Richard Whish, Wouter Wils, etc.

Online version

Concurrences website provides all articles published since its inception, in addition to selected articles published online only in the electronic supplement.

Write for Concurrences

Concurrences welcome spontaneous contributions. Except in rare circumstances, the journal accepts only unpublished articles, whatever the form and nature of the contribution. The Editorial Board checks the form of the proposals, and then submits these to the Scientific Committee. Selection of the papers is conditional to a peer review by at least two members of the Committee. Within a month, the Committee assesses whether the draft article can be published and notifies the author.

www.ingramcontent.com/pod-product-compliance
Lightning Source LLC
LaVergne TN
LVHW022043200926
848481LV00003B/766
* 9 7 8 1 9 5 4 7 5 0 9 3 7 *